THE **Sun-sation**

THE Sun-sation

BEHIND THE SCENES OF BRITAIN'S BESTSELLING DAILY NEWSPAPER

Roslyn Grose

ANGUS
& ROBERTSON
PUBLISHERS

Many thanks to all *The Sun* staff, both past and present, who so generously gave me their anecdotes and their time. Special thanks to *The Sun*'s excellent reference library for their patient help and to *Sun* picture librarian Don Beland for his painstaking research.

ANGUS & ROBERTSON PUBLISHERS

16 Golden Square, London W1R 4BN,
United Kingdom and
Unit 4, Eden Park, 31 Waterloo Road,
North Ryde, NSW, Australia 2113.

First published in the United Kingdom by
Angus & Robertson (UK) in 1989

Text copyright © Roslyn Grose 1989
Illustrations and photographs © News Group Newspapers 1989

British Library Cataloguing in Publication Data
Grose, Roslyn
    The SUN-sation – the inside story of Britain's
    bestselling daily newspaper.
    1. Newspapers with London imprints. Sun, The
    I. Title
    72'.1

ISBN 0 207 16384 7

Typeset in Great Britain by New Faces, Bedford
Printed in Great Britain by Scotprint Ltd., Musselburgh, Scotland

CONTENTS

Introduction

The Sun newspaper, biggest-selling daily paper in the English language, first rose with the dawn of 17 November 1969 and has been beaming over the breakfast tables of Britain ever since.

Outrageous, hard-hitting, hated by many but bought by millions, *The Sun* is now as much a fact of British life as the cuppa, the big red bus and the bobby on the beat. Consumed by a quarter of the adult population, it is impossible to ignore.

Its 12 million readers are addicted to the paper they have come to know as 'Your Number One Sun'. But many others loathe its head-butting editorial style and Thatcherite politics and like to claim that it has dragged the entire British tabloid press into the gutter.

Intellectuals find it beneath contempt, dismissing it as a tit-and-bum comic, not designed to be *read*. Attacking *The Sun* (known to those fond of it as 'the currant bun') is a popular sport among those who proudly boast that they don't read it themselves – a fact that somewhat weakens their argument.

But *The Sun* is not written for *Guardian* readers or eggheads who enjoy delicate debate. Its whole style is based on telling readers what they think – reflecting what is being said in pubs, on factory floors, in bus queues, behind counters and over back fences throughout the land.

A former assistant editor puts it this way: 'It's not a consensus paper. It says, "This is what we believe in – you're daft if you don't agree." And each day four and a quarter million buyers say, "We stand with you."'

Its language is colloquial and sometimes ungrammatical, often for the sake of making a headline fit the space available. Thus 'GOTCHA', the front-page splash during the height of Falklands fever, 'WHO TOLD THAT CHOPPER WHOPPER?' during the Westland helicopter row and 'YOU CHEEKY BEAS' when the Queen launched a witch-hunt into how the paper got hold of a private royal snap of tiny Princess Beatrice with her mother, grandmother and great-grandmother that was destined to be Her Majesty's Christmas card.

Sun puns are famous and have given the paper's sub-editors their reputation as the finest around. Among the more memorable are 'L'AMBUSH', on a story about the French hijacking of British lamb lorries; 'STRICTLY FOR CONNIE-SIRS', captioning a glamour picture of actress Stephanie Beacham star of the TV series, 'Connie'; 'I'VE GOT EWE UNDER MY SKIN' when it was revealed Frank Sinatra kept his youthful look with sheep implants.

Princess Diana has inspired dozens like 'HAPPY DI'S ARE HERE AGAIN', 'WHAT A DIFFERENCE A DI MAKES' and, the best headline that never actually appeared, 'DID DI DIDDLE THE ITIES?' suggested for a story that revealed the Princess was wearing old frocks on a visit to Italy.

'THE ION* LADY', complete with asterisk, was the front-page headline on a story about the Prime Minister's electric therapy treatments. It goes down as the first *Sun* headline that needed explanation.

The directness with which *The Sun* punches across its news stories and editorial messages is legend. Brevity is the key. A *Sun* writer will never use a word of two or more syllables if there is a single-syllable word with the same meaning. To prune the paper of unnecessary wordage, current editor Kelvin MacKenzie sent round a memo instructing that adjectives be left out of writers' copy.

THE Sun

Tuesday, May 4, 1982 14p TODAY'S TV: PAGE 12

QE2 IS SET TO SAIL FOR WAR

Liner may be turned back from a cruise

We told you first

GOTCHA

SUNK — AN Argie patrol boat like this one was sunk by missiles from Royal Navy helicopters after first opening fire on our lads

CRIPPLED — The Argie cruiser General Belgrano . . . put out of action by Tigerfish torpedoes from our super nuclear sub Conqueror

Our lads sink gunboat and hole cruiser

From TONY SNOW aboard HMS Invincible

THE NAVY had the Argies on their knees last night after a devastating double punch.

WALLOP: They torpedoed the 14,000-ton Argentine cruiser General Belgrano and left it a useless wreck.

WALLOP: Task Force helicopters sank another Argie patrol boat and severely damaged another.

UNION BOYCOTTS WAR

£50,000 BINGO! Today's lucky numbers are on P

THE Sun

£800 milko is just dirty crate cheat say wives

HRH IS NOT AMUSED

YOU CHEEKY BEAS

Sun THE QUEEN BEA

- Queen calls in lawyers
- We offer to return photo

The Queen . . . ordered an inquiry

TTO—Page 11 ● £31,000 BINGO—Page 20

THE Sun

Thursday, January 16, 1986 18p TODAY'S TV: PAGE 12

Dallas sensation
MY AIDS FEAR
By SUE ELLEN
See Centre Pages

WESTLAND: The Sun asks the vital question

WHO TOLD THAT CHOPPER WHOPPER?

WAS IT HIM? **OR WAS IT HIM?**

By TREVOR KAVANAGH
Political Editor

Sun news special

£40,000 TWINGO BINGO! Today's lucky numbers—See Page 19

Experts have estimated that *The Sun* never demands a reading age of more than twelve, with its simple straightforward language, short sentences, short stories. This does produce obvious jokes about the IQ and literacy of *Sun* readers – but clearly a quarter of Britain's adults *don't* move their lips and run their fingers under the words as they read.

The paper's succinct, racy style is not only appreciated by its readers but admired by those in the business of communication. Getting the message across to the maximum number of people is the goal and *The Sun* has beaten all opposition in the tabloid battle.

As a reflection of its powers of communication, it has been known for those preparing government information leaflets for, say, the Department of Health and Social Security, to call *The Sun*'s editorial offices for help with their phrasing.

The paper's approach is well illustrated by the 'Twenty Things You Never Knew About . . .' formula which serves up a rag-bag of facts about any person or topic in the news. It sprung up in response to the editor's mania for updating the paper's stories so close to deadline times that writers could barely pound out the words in the seconds left, let alone produce polished copy.

A writer was struggling at the last minute with a fast analysis of what was going on in the Persian Gulf. Faced with a mountain of facts, there was barely time to string sentences together and certainly no space for words like 'meanwhile'. A woman features executive suggested, almost as a joke, the 'Twenty Things' format. It has been part of the paper's distinctive style ever since, turning up on the sports pages, in television coverage, political reports and on the pop and showbiz pages. It is the ideal tabloid solution to the problem of piling facts into limited space.

It has been copied and spoofed mercilessly as a way of trivializing news issues. But as one *Sun* man put it, '"Twenty Things" is as much journalism as Bernard Levin. It is just a way of delivering facts in McNugget-style portions.'

The Sun's success story is a colourful one. Starting at the bottom of the tabloids' league table twenty years ago, it rose relentlessly to its present unchallenged position as Britain's favourite daily newspaper. Love it or loathe it, it is here to stay, causing such an impact that other papers are frequently forced to report its activities. When *The Sun* gets into trouble with royalty, the law or a particular section of the community, opposition papers have a field day. And this seems to cause more people to go out and buy a copy, out of curiosity.

Even those not actually tempted to fork out twenty-two pence to find out what horror *The Sun* has committed or what scandal the paper has uncovered will often write to the newspaper to complain about a story they have not read. They may see a headline flash in front of them on television, in a news item concerning the paper, or the paper being waved about in a studio discussion. And as a result they are moved to send off an angry letter.

Stirring up reaction is what newspapers are all about. *The Sun* leaves the competition standing.

1. *Sunrise*

The birth of *The Sun* as we know it was in fact the rebirth of what had been a rather dull broadsheet of the same name that had struggled for five years during the Swinging Sixties to establish itself as a middle-of-the-road Labour paper in the Mirror Group.

By 1969 it was selling only about 850,000 copies a day. It had lost more than 12 million pounds since the *Mirror* bought it from the TUC in 1961 when it was known as the *Daily Herald*. Consequently, the *Mirror*'s Hugh Cudlipp thought he did well to off-load the ailing paper's title to the fresh young Fleet Street proprietor from Down Under, Rupert Murdoch.

Murdoch, who had bought the *News of the World* the year before, got *The Sun* for the bargain price of £600,000. It gave him a daily paper to print on his Sunday paper's presses, then idle from Sunday to Friday.

Today, he explains why he took up the challenge, which looked like an act of madness to many at the time: 'It certainly wasn't affection for *The Sun*, it was determination to challenge the *Daily Mirror*. I felt it had lost touch with the younger generation and that there was a great opportunity there.

'I considered starting up from scratch. I considered buying the old *Daily Sketch* from Lord Rothermere – but he wouldn't give me a yes or no. Then I had this wild idea of *The Sun*.

'It was very open to doubt whether it was better than a clean start-up. But we felt there was some sort of base there, some old readers and an existing name which made it a little more secure.'

Next he went shopping for an editor. He outlined the requirements: 'I am looking for someone who is young, enthusiastic, hungry, ambitious, tough and likeable enough to carry the staff with him.'

He found Larry Lamb, a gifted, ambitious, forty-year-old Yorkshireman who was then northern editor of the *Daily Mail*. They had talks about the kind of paper the revamped *Sun* should be – and discovered they were made for each other. 'We had virtually identical concepts,' Lamb said later.

The shiny new *Sun*'s leader writer and columnist, Henry Russell Douglas, remembers his new editor outlining his vision of the paper: 'He thought we should aim for what the *Daily Mirror* had been in the Fifties before it lost its way and became pompous. It used to be outspoken and sometimes outrageous, a left-wing newspaper ready to shout its mouth off at anything it thought ought to be shouted at. But it had become a bit Establishment, perhaps because we had a Labour government. Generally, they had lost their devil-may-care attitude and ability to surprise.'

The Murdoch *Sun* was expected to hit the streets in March 1970. But the public and indeed the *Sun* staff got their first big surprise when the paper's new owner decided to go for an early launch.

Murdoch says now, 'There was some controversy over whether we would let the old *Sun* close down then re-start. But the fact was, we had bought it, it would have been a nonsense to have a day filled by another title.'

The old *Sun* would finish publishing at the end of one week and the new one would appear the following Monday.

'I joined on 13 October 1969, the same day as Larry got there,' says Douglas. 'One day shortly afterwards, Rupert said to Larry that the old *Sun* was running down so fast there would be nothing left to found a new paper on. He asked, what would it look like if we started it the following month?'

Pretty rough, was Larry Lamb's estimate. 'We wouldn't be very proud of it.'

Murdoch then asked if it would be worse than the *Daily Sketch,* a now-defunct downmarket tabloid.

A slightly indignant Larry Lamb said no, of course it wouldn't be worse than that.

'Right,' said Murdoch, 'we'll start on 17 November.'

The rush was on. And there were plenty of problems due to shortage of staff and lack of tabloid experience on both the editorial and production sides. Many of the staff had switched overnight from the old to the new *Sun* with little or no time for briefings on what was wanted.

Ex-*Mirror* man Brian McConnell was one of the few with tabloid know-how – the skills involved in making the most impact with the least words.

'Most of our people are first-rate broadsheet writers but in tabloids the appraisal – and the length – is different,' he was explaining in the first week of publication, as writers used to filling acres of space were suddenly confined to cramming the same amount of information into half the column inches.

Glamour photographer Beverley Goodway, who now takes all *The Sun*'s Page Three photographs, was one who came from the old *Sun.* He remembers: 'It was bizarre. On the last week of the old paper I was in their studio shooting fashion pictures of footballer Bobby Moore's wife for the following week's start of Murdoch's *Sun.*'

A new telephone exchange installed in the Bouverie Street offices of the new *Sun* was not fully functional and as engineers worked among the reporters', sub-editors' and copytakers' desks, correspondents hanging on the end of phones all over the country were waiting for up to an hour to dictate their copy.

There were no dummy runs. Normally, when a new publication is about to be launched, dummy copies are produced to give everyone the chance to see and polish the end product. But there was no time for that – the first issue of *The Sun* was the dummy. The nearest the machine-room got to a run-through on the unfamiliar presses was when they gathered together some waste type left over from the *News of the World* and zapped out ten pages.

Everyone had to learn as they went along. But everyone loved it and goodwill abounded. One night the hard-pressed machine room was given a hand by *Daily Telegraph* staff who gave up their meal break to help get the paper off.

Some staff worked up to eighteen hours a day and twelve hour shifts were commonplace. Editor Larry Lamb told *UK Press Gazette*, the newspaper industry's trade journal: 'The staff have been marvellous. They are all hollow-eyed and working their guts out.'

Even Rupert Murdoch pitched in alongside the editor, deputy editor Bernard Shrimsley and assistant editor Norman Baitey to work as stone subs – those who make the last-minute adjustments to hot metal before the presses roll. The joke was that they were the highest paid stone subs in Fleet Street.

Murdoch's comment at the end of the first week was simply: 'It's bloody chaos – but we are getting a newspaper out.'

One executive said: 'There's an open-door policy here. A successful paper gets bogged down with Establishment thinking. Here we have no time. The old enthusiasm is back, people are proud of their job.'

For Bernard Shrimsley, current associate editor of the *Daily Express*, the experience was 'unmatched and unmatchable'. He says now, 'We all had something to prove. I was editor of the *Liverpool Post*, Larry was northern editor of the *Daily Mirror*, there were key people from the old *Sun*. We were all looking for the chance to prove what we thought we could do. It was a wonderful fluke that that team came together. If you had taken any one or two away from the nucleus you might not have got the same result.

'It must have been rather like the discovery of the atom bomb: all the bits clicked at the same time. The result was Hiroshima. In Bouverie Street it was *The Sun*. There was non-stop excitement in the office and it came through to the paper.'

A young features sub-editor in those first days was Deidre Sanders, later to return as the paper's agony aunt. She was working on the rather trendy, upmarket women's magazine, *Nova*, and answered the call for subs to do night shifts in Bouverie Street.

'I used to walk out of the calm *Nova* atmosphere into the completely frantic scene at *The Sun*,' she recalls. 'It was tremendous fun, uplifting. I was about twenty-four and full of the thrill of getting to Fleet Street.

'We worked in a long room like a corridor which was very brown and grubby. And you got everything thrown at you – the stars, a book serialization. You did everything by the seat of your pants. As a young journalist it was a fantastic way of building up nerve and judgement. There was so much energy around, it crackled.

'It was all sleeves rolled up and getting stuck in. And it had a real feeling of being good. *The Sun* had a feeling of attack and grip and it showed right from the start.'

When the paper's first issue – a fat forty-eight pages with 'HORSE DOPE SENSATION' as its front-page lead story – came off the presses, it looked a bit of a mess to expert eyes.

Editor Larry Lamb was bitterly disappointed, to the point where he felt he had 'botched the job'. In *The Sun*'s eighteenth birthday issue in 1987, he wrote:

> The new newspaper was so rough at the edges that the word 'crude', a description much beloved of the pundits at that time, looked like a wholly objective assessment.
>
> And the paper was late. Disastrously so. When my wife drove home with Mr Murdoch and his wife Anna, early on the morning of the 17th, I think we were all close to tears.

Bernard Shrimsley remembers joking to his boss, 'Another night like this, Rupert, and I'm going back to Australia.'

He also remembers Rupert Murdoch's wife, Anna, going up to a couple of machine-room men in their overalls and asking, 'What do you do?' Their reply was, 'We're the workers.'

'She said to them, "See that little guy in his short-sleeves – he's a worker too." It was Rupert.'

Henry Russell Douglas describes that night's paper: 'We were fairly appalled. We had cobbled it together terribly quickly and it showed

on that first number. There were a lot of rough edges.

'But I personally have thought since that the rough edges were to our advantage. It seemed different and not a beautifully packaged deal like the others. It had an immediacy which set it apart.'

There was a mixed reaction from the rest of the media, ranging from indulgent pats on the head and mutterings of 'Good try' from some quarters to outrage and hostility from others.

There was something in issue No. 1 for everyone. Apart from the horse-doping scandal on page one, there was a picture of Lady Leonora Grosvenor above the headline. 'Where are Charles and Lady

Leonora?' – a story about twenty-one-year-old Prince Charles' latest rumoured romance. There was an interview with Prime Minister Harold Wilson in which he attacked the Tories over their plans to introduce VAT. There was a pretty girl on Page Three, her curves well covered by a baggy shirt, with a caption that emphasized her more-than-just-a-pretty-face appeal: 'This Swedish charmer has a nice line in brains, too. At present she's studying to become a systems analyst for computers in Stockholm.'

From 'the book every woman wants to read' – *The Love Machine* by Jacqueline Susann – there was part one of a series of extracts. Australia's top cartoonist Paul Rigby blasted off with a witty comment on America's Apollo 12 moonwards launch. Liz Taylor was shown turning up at a party with her latest out-size diamond.

The women's pages claimed to be 'for women who believe there is more to life than washing up'. Among other things they were promised a free knitting pattern.

The fashion page had 'Undies for Undressing'. And there was both sex and rock-and-roll on a double-page spread showing Mick Jagger and the rest of The Rolling Stones with an undressed groupie.

For sports fans there was 'The George Best Page' on soccer. And for the kids, a 'Super soccer wall chart' to send for, after which they could save coupons printed daily in the paper till they had enough for a free set of stick-on club crests. (This was a brilliant promotional wheeze, known as 'the apron tug', which made young children nag their parents to buy the paper.)

The next day *The Times* gave its verdict:

> Mr Murdoch's new *Sun* has done its best to resurrect the *Daily Mirror* of the 1930s in order to compete with the *Daily Mirror* of the 1970s. Its formula is a simple one: it is the formula of sex, sport and sensation and Mr Murdoch could fairly borrow from Schweppes and call his paper the S-s-sun. This is an old way to create a new paper.
>
> As a brash tabloid *The Sun* shows considerable technical achievement. It has been put together at great speed, with

insufficient time for preparation, and with a small staff . . .
the production is highly professional.

It will be interesting to see whether the new *Sun* is a
commercial success. It very well could be. Mr Murdoch has
not invented sex but he does show a remarkable enthusiasm
for its benefits to circulation, such as a tired old Fleet Street
has not seen in recent years.

The *Morning Star* was rather less enthusiastic. It ranted:

Mr Rupert Murdoch's first effort yesterday was less like a
sun than a paraffin lamp in a brothel. It cast virtually no light
on the great problems of the world and of Britain, and on
the hopes and aspirations of our people.

. . . Those who want to see the way forward out of our
difficulties, those who want a working-class view of the
world rather than a brash millionaire's opinion of what the
working-class ought to want, will get no help from *The Sun.*

While it did not go unnoticed that *The Sun* was aiming straight at
the *Mirror*'s market, even to the point of stealing its slogan, 'Forward
with the people', those in charge at the *Mirror* showed no sign of
worry. After all, that newspaper's daily sale was 4,250,000 at the time.

On the evening that issue No. 1 of *The Sun* rolled off the press,
Hugh Cudlipp held a party at the International Publishing
Corporation's headquarters. The room where the owners of the *Daily
Mirror* and previous owners of *The Sun* raised their glasses was
decorated with withered sunflowers. Cudlipp's reaction to the new
arrival, which was delivered hot off the press in the middle of the
party, was said to be: 'That's no threat to anybody.'

He could not have been more wrong, *The Sun* never looked like a
loser. On the third day of publication they claimed sales of 1,650,000
copies – nearly double the circulation of the old *Sun*. And that was
despite the deadline and delivery chaos which meant that some places
in Britain did not actually see *The Sun* till 10.00am on its first day.

'We hardly got it out at all the first night – yet it sold immediately,' Rupert Murdoch recalls.

Within three months the regular daily sale was 1.5 million and *The Sun* soared in popularity from then on.

Jubilantly, it chalked up its birthdays and milestones, at first in days:

> Believe it or not, we're 21 today. This is the 21st issue of the new-style *Sun*. It its present format *The Sun* is still a baby. But what a bouncing baby. AND WE DON'T INTEND TO LOSE ANY OF THE BOUNCE NOW WE HAVE COME OF AGE.

Then it reached 100:

> Meet Britain's liveliest centenarian. Today *The Sun* is 100 issues old.
>
> There won't be a telegram from Buckingham Palace. But there will be close on 4,000,000 guests at the party. Our readers. The people who count.

By this time the rest of the media was starting to accept that the soaraway *Sun* was here to stay.

'This is a paper which knows where it is going. It knows what kind of readers it is after and it knows or gives the impression of knowing how to get them,' said 'BBC News Stand'.

'This new *Sun* is a fantastic thing. Rupert Murdoch is showing Fleet Street a bit of professionalism,' said the circulation manager of the *London Evening Standard*.

The *Financial Times* acknowledged: '*The Sun*'s success is undoubted'.

And there had not yet even been a bare-breasted beauty on Page Three.

2. Page Three Has Its Knockers

Every newspaper has a page three. But mention it and most people will presume you are talking about that page of *The Sun*, the place where, six days a week, you are guaranteed to find a pretty girl wearing little more than a smile.

Even those who say they have never seen *The Sun* will often smirk in acknowledgement of the fact that to most of Britain, Page Three means only one thing – *The Sun*'s topless pin-ups.

It is easy to say that this daily dose of titillation is what sells the paper. But clearly it does not. Other newspapers have jumped on the Page Three bandwagon without noticeable leaps in circulation. Some have tried going further by giving us girls in colour (the 'Starbirds', for example) and less far by carefully covering the girls' bare essentials (as in the *Daily Mirror*).

Page Three is a vital part of *The Sun*'s successful package, but editor Kelvin MacKenzie believes 'Page Three is no more important than Hagar the Horrible.' (Hagar is a monstrous Viking who stars in the paper's back-page comic strip).

It does raise higher passions, however, than Hagar. Banning Page Three from the walls of factories and offices, locking the paper out of local libraries and attacking it for exploiting women as sex objects have all been favourite occupations among those who disapprove on grounds of prudery or sexism.

During *The Sun's* first year there was not a nipple to be seen, though Page Three was always the paper's beauty spot. The girls then tended to be actresses rather than models, often pictured at photo calls for whatever West End play, TV show or film they were about to adorn.

True, they wore as little as possible – but not little enough to excite Mary Whitehouse. The roll-call of Page Three actresses is fascinating to look back on: Kate O'Mara was there, so were Britt Ekland, Stephanie Beacham, Jill St John, Madeline Smith, Samantha Eggar, Anthea Redfern, Swedish Julie Ege and Italian Virna Lisi.

Sprinkled among them were dozens of unknown Australian bathing beauties. There was thought to be nothing like the sight of a smiling girl in a swimsuit, photographed in the sunshine, to cheer up a British commuter on a winter morning when the trains weren't running too well.

Photographer Beverley Goodway, *The Sun's* most famous snapper of glamour pictures, says he has never received an instruction on what was wanted since those early days when the brief was simply to get pretty girls in the paper.

'In the late Sixties, fashion was the rage and it was the way to get more girls in the paper. There were endless photo calls which you went to, not for the clothes but the chance of snapping the girls.

'I can remember going round Paris trying to get tall, flat-chested French models to smile – but they just didn't want to know.'

The nipple barrier was broken by an unidentified model whose naked torso stretched horizontally across a page of *The Sun* and who was topless in more ways than one: her head was cropped from the picture. But she was an advertisement – for Formica. The picture caption dreamed up by the admen read: 'The second most interesting surface in the world'.

That was hardly shocking. It should be remembered that shows like *Hair* and *Oh! Calcutta!* were pulling in the crowds in the West End – even Princess Anne went to *Hair*. And in the south of France, it was becoming the norm to go topless on the beach.

A *Sun* photographer on assignment in the Mediterranean sent back a set of pictures of pretty girl holidaymakers. One in particular caught the eye of picture editor Len Hickman and editor Larry Lamb: she was topless, but lying in the water with the waves washing round her.

'Will we or won't we?' they agonized.

The picture was a subtle step forward, 'Is she or isn't she? Now you see them, not you don't,' was the muted reaction.

There were no such doubts when the paper decided to go for it on its first birthday. On 17 November 1970, Page Three featured its first 'birthday suit' girl, model Stephanie Rahn, bare as the day she was born, tastefully photographed sitting sideways in long grass.

In today's terms the caption was most peculiar. It was uncharacteristically defensive for a paper with a brash reputation. It read:

> From time to time some self-appointed critic stamps his tiny foot and declares that *The Sun* is obsessed with sex. It is not *The Sun*, but the critics, who are obsessed. *The Sun*, like most of its readers, likes pretty girls.

Rupert Murdoch, away in Australia at the time, says he was just as shocked as anybody else when he saw it. 'It was a daring experiment,' he says on reflection. 'But it swiftly became a national institution. It was a statement of youthfulness and freshness.'

After that, topless Page Three girls became a regular feature of *The Sun*.

It was a relief to photographers who no longer had to pretend it was a fashion or showbiz story they were after. 'We could come clean,' says photographer Goodway.

In those days, when anyone with an sense of adventure was desperate to be a paid-up member of the so-called 'permissive society', Page Three pictures were far more blatantly sexy than they are today. Girls posed with legs apart, hands aggressively on hips, breasts thrust at the camera, lips wet and pouting. They stood under showers with their nipples erect, they glistened with body oil.

They were outrageous and there were some predictable reactions. Like the engineering firm in Bury, Lancashire, which insisted on the removal of a Page Three pin-up of a judge's daughter, Kathy McKinnon, before a visit from the Duke of Kent.

Judge's daughter, Kathy McKinnon

Of course, the duke's private secretary said afterwards he was sure the duke would not have minded seeing the picture. 'He's been a soldier for years. Do you think he's never seen this sort of thing before?'

Some objections were funnier. An exotic Page Three favourite called Vanya inspired bosses at the Marconi Radar Systems factory in Leicester to poetic heights when they penned this message to workers:

> Vanya, dear Vanya,
> We are sorry to ban ya,
> But displaying your charms
> On occasion alarms,
> And in areas of science,
> Upsets visiting clients.

To which the workers replied:

> We put her on our factory wall
> She lasted half an hour,
> The management removed her –
> Narrow-minded shower.

Then there was the saga of Sowerby Bridge in Yorkshire, where the library committee decided *The Sun* was 'too sexy' for the reading room and decided to ban it. This inspired the headline, 'The silly burghers of Sowerby Bridge'. That was followed by a visit to the town by *The Sun's* columnist, Jon Akass, who began his piece: 'We should be thrown out of better places than this'.

When the library persisted with its ban, the paper hit back by running a contest, 'Win a free weekend in Sowerby Bridge'. The winner, from Lichfield, Staffordshire, turned it down with the words, 'Don't be daft. I was born there.'

Politicians got involved. When Kent libraries stopped their readers seeing Page Three by cutting out popular papers to keep costs down,

Thanet East's Tory MP Jonathan Aitken was deluged with protest letters. 'This decision is ridiculous,' he said. 'Everybody has a right to see Page Three girls. Put them back!'

Labour MPs were usually more inclined to want to ban the page. During a debate on an indecency bill, Alexander Lyon, MP for York, claimed: 'On Page Three there is a semi-nude woman which could give offence to somebody sitting opposite in a crowded bus or train. If someone took exception to its contents, it might be right for *The Sun* or the newsagents to be prosecuted.'

Page Three has changed since those days – and so have the protests.

Beverley Goodway tells his side of it: 'Because I have never been given any brief about what sort of pictures to take, I have always worked out what's wanted by what goes in the paper. We used to have a lot of legs-apart, face-to-the-camera stuff where the sexier ones were not the smiling ones. Lately I've noticed the pretty-pretty smiling ones get chosen. There's a demand for the approachable girl-next-door who is prettier, more homely.

The reaction sought now is not: 'Cor, look at her.' I wouldn't like to use the word 'coy' but perhaps that's right. Today the mood is gentler, it's more about pretty faces than it used to be.'

Glib critics refer to *The Sun*'s glamour approach as 'tit-and-bum'. Beverley reckons 'face-and-boobs' is more accurate. There are few full-length pictures.

Young girls rush to be on Page Three. And where once it was a source of family embarrassment, now their mothers, brothers, boyfriends and neighbours often write to *The Sun* on the girls' behalf. Beverley says, 'We are deluged'.

There are few worries, it seems, about fronting up in the altogether before a strange male photographer. But this may be because of family man Goodway's ambiguous first name – Beverley is frequently presumed to be female.

He tells the story of a man heard boasting in a Manchester pub about his girlfriend's success on Page Three: 'The blokes finished up by saying that his girl was making a fortune but she had to give it up ''because that Beverley Goodway is a lesbian''.'

The photographer also gets lots of mail from women talking about their bodies in the light of the girls they see in the paper. Nine out of ten times they begin: 'I know you'll understand, as a woman . . .'

He does, however, encourage girls who come to be photographed the first time to bring their mum or boyfriend along 'to see it is all professional and not all terribly seedy'.

On the reverse side of the coin, Beverley has had the odd bad moment – like the time he had to call for help to get one hopeful model out of the studio.

'She was bigger than me,' says the slightly-built Goodway, 'and she kept disappearing to the loo where I suspect she was sniffing, smoking or swallowing something. I took a couple of rolls of film to keep her happy, then she grabbed me by the tie and said, ''Is that all you want?''

'I was so alarmed I phoned the office for help. They all fell about. Then they sent a news photographer round – with his camera. I found it a completely unnerving experience.'

Not any pretty girl who takes her clothes off is necessarily right for the job. 'You can't just walk into a studio and make it happen. Girls who succeed have polished their hair, their make-up, their skin,' says Beverley.

'I look for a good figure and pretty face, confidence, personality and polish – a word I over-use. Grooming is important, by which I mean an ability to glow.'

One girl who just walked off the street within days of her sixteenth birthday was Samantha Fox, a five-foot-nothing pneumatic blonde who had been thrown out of school for posing topless for a newspaper.

'I wasn't that convinced at the start. But she just got better and better. She got her make-up and looks so right so quickly, you couldn't ignore her.'

Sam was voted the readers' favourite 'Page Three Girl of the Year' for three years in succession and is now, at twenty-three, an established recording star with fans worldwide. She has proved

Samantha Fox, aged sixteen, in her first Page Three appearance

beyond doubt that Page Three is a stepping stone to stardom and riches.

Another all-time favourite is Linda Lusardi, a slim brunette whose dazzling smile has endeared her to the British public far more than measurable assets ever could. Just before her thirtieth birthday, *Sun* readers voted her their favourite for the year. A year later they named her 'Page Three Girl of the Decade' in a telephone poll. She is now making a successful career as a stage actress.

Yesterday's starlets are clearly today's Page Three hopefuls. If a girl becomes a favourite with *Sun* readers it makes her a household name. The paper then starts featuring her as a personality in gossip items. If she gets a new man in her life, buys a house or a flash car, it makes news.

Once she is recognized, even with her clothes on, by about 12 million *Sun* readers, a girl is immediately in demand for public appearances in discos and supermarkets all over Britain – at several hundred pounds a time.

When nineteen-year-old Maria Whittaker was crowned 'Page Three Girl of the Year' in September 1988 she reckoned the boost in her earnings from those personal appearances could make a million pounds by her twenty-first birthday.

Sun glamour photographer Steve Lewis sums up what Page Three means to the girls when he says: 'You can take a girl from an ordinary background, put her in *The Sun* two or three times, then she gets whisked away to the Philippines, say, on a calendar shoot with Patrick Lichfield.

'The exposure they get in *The Sun* can set girls up for life. Maria Whittaker came from a pre-fabricated home on the flight path at Heathrow. Now she lives with her boyfriend in a half-million-pound house in Essex.'

Few girls have second thoughts about the impact their pictures have and most are mystified by accusations that what they are doing degrades women. They will tell you of the letters they get from women, asking for make-up, beauty or diet tips. They are mostly horrified by any suggestion that by appearing undressed in a newspaper they may cause a man to go out and commit a sex crime.

'If I thought that was true, I would never do it again,' a shocked Page Three girl told a TV audience last year.

Beverley Goodway, as the father of two young teenage girls, says he has worried over the possibility that a Page Three picture could be an incitement to rape. There is no direct evidence that this is so and he finds it hard to believe.

'The pictures are just very pretty and cute. If the girl had her clothes on, blokes would get equally steamed up.'

Labour MP Clare Short fought a losing battle to have *The Sun*'s Page Three and other newspaper nudes banned with her Indecent Displays (Newspapers) Bill, a private members Bill she tried to get through Parliament in 1986.

She described Page Three as 'blatant and crude' and said it gave her a feeling of revulsion, shared by hundreds of other women who had written to her in support. The pictures degraded women, she said. And while admitting there was no evidence linking pictures of naked women with cases of rape, she could not believe they were never an incitement.

The only Page Three girl publicly to regret her career as a topless model was Geraldine June, who last went before the cameras more than ten years ago. She wrote a full-page piece about her change of heart in *Cosmopolitan* magazine in January 1989.

'I would not like the responsibility of linking pin-ups to sex crimes,' she wrote. 'But neither do we need a dossier on baked beans to prove than an advertisement encourages us to buy a tin.'

No doubt there will always be arguments over Page Three. But those who wish to ban it are unlikely to succeed in getting the girls to cover up.

Apart from the fact that very few people feel it is an issue to lose sleep over, how could you possibly legislate against it? To outlaw Page Three girls in *The Sun*, you would also have to ban the nudes in *Vogue*, cover up half the statues in our parks and gardens and remove all the naked ladies in the National Gallery from public view.

The history of the pin-up goes back centuries, since man first painted the female form unadorned. Page Three girls are simply the late twentieth century version, made available via modern technology to millions instead of a select few.

3. *The Sun Says*

When you read a *Sun* editorial – 'The Sun Says' – it is like being kicked by a steel-capped boot. There's no messing about with esoteric argument, no nonsense about 'on the one hand . . . but then on the other . . .'

Sun editorials are famous for their direct-hit policy. They are also now renowned for their firm right-wing stance – indeed, since Mrs Thatcher became prime minister ten years ago, what 'The Sun Says' is generally thought to be indistinguishable from what the prime minister says. 'Maggie's mouthpiece' is how some left-wingers bitterly refer to *The Sun*.

Perhaps surprisingly, when *The Sun* covered its first general election nearly twenty years ago, it was firmly in favour of the Labour party. Its election eve editorial of 17 June 1970, headed 'Why It Must Be Labour' read:

> In the past few weeks The Sun has kept its promise to bring you all the Election news. Our coverage has been, as we promised, detailed, analytical and non-partisan. We also promised that we would tell you, when the time came, which way The Sun would vote. The time has come, and The Sun would vote Labour.

Not because the Government has been a scintillating success. It hasn't.

But because, all things considered, we think that Harold Wilson has the better team. Not only the better team, but a team which is fundamentally more concerned about ordinary people. Concerned, too, about things like social justice, equality of opportunity and the quality of living. These are the things The Sun cares about. The Sun believes that Edward Heath cares about them too. But we feel that they are more likely to be lost sight of under a Tory administration. For Mr Heath is not the Tory Party. And The Sun is not convinced that the Tory Leopard has changed its spots.

For everyone who cares about these things, tomorrow is the moment of decision. In the House of Commons on April 23 this year (*Hansard*, column 633), the Prime Minister said: 'However tired people may be of me, I think that most people will regard me as the lesser of the two evils.' And he added: 'I always put these things in a modest way.'

The Sun's verdict is that the Prime Minister is right.

Labour lost.

On 27 February 1974, the eve of the next election, *The* Sun headed its message to the voters 'The Devil And The Deep Blue Sea'.

What in the name of Great Britain should we be voting for tomorrow?

The Sun believes that there is one issue which matters more than all the rest put together: Getting Britain out of the red. The party that ought to rule is the party with the guts to do what must be done to work us out of the colossal mess we are in. Last year The Sun warned that we could not go on living on tick, paying ourselves more than we earned. Last month The Sun said the Election had to be on this issue before all others. Last week we called for honesty, from any party or from all of them, about how grim the immediate prospects are. We are still waiting. Like many millions of voters, The Sun does not find it easy to make up its mind about this difficult General Election. To choose between the devil and the deep blue sea.

After a run-down of the two major parties' prospects, *The Sun* reached its conclusion:

> Reluctantly, and as a choice of evils, The Sun believes that on this occasion, in the straight fight between Labour and the Tories, it is the Tories who must get its vote.

The Tories lost that one. They also lost the second general election that year, in October. *The Sun* gave up in despair that time, headlining its pre-election editorial, on 8 October 1974, 'May The Best Men Win – And Heaven Help Us If They Don't'. It wrote:

> The Sun believes that, though the people have little enthusiasm for the personalities, they understand the issues very well. There are only two that matter: galloping inflation and the sinister, ever-growing power of a small band of anarchists, bully-boys and professional class-war warriors. Or, to put it another way, we're flat broke, and our democracy is in real danger. With neither the Tories nor the Labour Party telling us the whole truth; with neither putting forward anything effective in the way of new policies; with the Liberals high on enthusiasm, being woefully lacking in talent and experience, how can we support any party? The Sun, if it had a vote this vital Thursday, would vote not for the best manifesto but for the best man or woman.

The best man turned out to be Harold Wilson and *The Sun* went along with that. In an editorial on 9 May 1975 exhorting the prime minister to sack 'Her Majesty's disastrous Secretary of State for

Flood Street, 1975: Margaret Thatcher puts on her power make-up

Industry Mr Anthony Wedgwood ("Citizen") Benn,' *The Sun* said:

> The Sun, not for the first time, has some advice for the Prime
> Minister, who is still the best Prime Minister we've got.
>   It is this:
> Don't clip Wedgie's wings.
> Don't transfer him to another department.
> Don't rap his knuckles with a feather duster.
> Sack him, Harold! For all our sakes. Not least for yours.

But by the next general election, on 3 May 1979, *The Sun* had
reached a decision about the Labour party.

The paper's owner, Rupert Murdoch, says now, 'We were all
Labour-inclined when we started *The Sun* but I think we grew pretty
disillusioned along with the rest of the country.'

The Sun's **front page** was entirely devoted to telling its readers how
to vote:

> A message to Labour supporters
> VOTE TORY THIS TIME
> It's the only way to stop the rot.

That was the paper's main headline, alongside a 'Page One
Opinion' piece headed 'The first day of the rest of our lives.' It said:

> This is D-Day. D for Decision. The first day of the rest of our
> lives.
>   The Sun today wishes particularly to address itself to
> traditional supporters of the Labour Party, and to those who
> have not hitherto had the opportunity to vote in a General
> Election.
>   We are particularly well-qualified so to do.
>   The roots of The Sun are planted deep among the working
> class.
>   We are proud to have a working class readership. The

LARGEST working class readership of any daily paper.

We are equally proud of the fact that we have more young readers than any of our contemporaries.

Both young people and traditional Labour Party supporters tend to be idealists. And The Sun is an idealistic newspaper.

We firmly believe in that system of Government which offers the greatest good to the greatest number.

That is precisely why, on this momentous occasion, we firmly advise our readers to VOTE TORY.

The Sun is not a Tory newspaper.

Indeed, alone among popular national newspapers, it can safely lay claim to being independent.

We have, at various times, advised our readers to vote for Labour, to vote for the Tories and to vote for the best man regardless of party.

The reasons for voting Tory filled page two, which concluded:

We believe that today's note must be for hope. For aspiration. For the young. For compassion. For thrust.

The Sun says: Vote Tory. Stop the Rot. There may not be another chance.

That editorial, written by editor Larry Lamb with leader writer Ronald Spark (newly hired to write editorials backing Tory case) was felt by many to have played a strong part in Mrs Thatcher's runaway victory.

'At Tory Central office, they considered The Sun crucial to their campaign,' Spark admits. 'Maggie saw Larry and at times Murdoch because they felt the Tories were best for their readers.'

In particular, it was the new-style Tories like grocer's daughter Margaret Thatcher and grammar-school boy Norman Tebbit who appealed to The Sun. 'Murdoch felt the Tories should make the break with the old school tie, the people with an inherited right to govern,' says Ronald Spark.

That explains his editorial of 10 June 1983, just after the Tories had yet again swept to victory. Headed 'WHY MAGGIE MUST GIVE PYM THE PUSH', it said:

> The Foreign Secretary typifies the wets, the people who want it all ways. A comfy seat in the Cabinet, but the right to distance themselves from any unpopular decision.
>
> . . . Master Pym, Jim Prior, Waffling Willie Whitelaw contributed nothing to the Tory victory. They were content to cling to the Prime Minister's petticoats.
>
> She owes them nothing. Except the door.

Boss Murdoch is no great lover of the royal family or the Establishment. He explains: 'I'm a bit sceptical. I don't perhaps hold in awe the British institutions that other people do. I guess it's my Australian background coming out. I'm from the new world where we have egalitarian traditions. We don't have class-ridden, out-of-date English decadence.'

'Basically Murdoch is a republican who sees the royal family as the peak of the class system which does a great deal of harm,' says Spark who is in total agreement and therefore does not hesitate to bash the royals whenever he feels they deserve it.

One of his best efforts was on 20 August 1987 under the headline 'Stop that thinking!' in which he referred to an interesting revelation about Prince Charles.

> Prince Charles does not want to be King.
>
> This is the most fascinating disclosure in Judy Wade's fascinating series in The Sun.
>
> One day he will inherit the Throne. At this stage, there is little he can do about it.
>
> That is sad for Charles.
>
> *Maybe it is also sad for the country.*
>
> Charles is moderately intelligent. He is conscientious. He also thinks a good deal.
>
> Would that necessarily be a good thing for Britain?
>
> People who think often also wish to act.
>
> If the sovereign imagines he has real power he comes to grief.
>
> In modern times, the best rulers of Britain have been dim.
>
> GEORGE VI never tried to interfere, except once when he lectured the BBC on the pronunciation of 'equerry'.
>
> GEORGE V was happiest collecting stamps and massacring birds.
>
> EDWARD VII ate eight-course breakfasts and chased women.
>
> Among the more intelligent Kings who wanted to do things . . .

CHARLES I lost his head.
CHARLES II sold his country to the French.
GEORGE III lost America.
So what's the best choice for Charles? Either stop thinking or make way for his kids.

If they turn out to be too bright, how about his brother Andrew?
His head seems to be merely a place for his Navy cap!

Spark says he is never told what to write by his proprietor and indeed, earlier *Sun* leader writers agree there was never any interference from Murdoch. However, they were made aware of his views by their editors.

'I don't remember any occasion when Rupert directly intervened,' says Henry Russell Douglas. 'But I had an idea that when Larry Lamb told me a line that had to be taken, at the back of my mind I thought, 'that's Rupert's instructions.'

The boss himself describes his in-put as 'spasmodic', while admitting, 'Some people will tell you I underestimate my own influence.'

In a four-column leader on 6 February 1989 *The Sun* spoke its mind on the defeated Privacy Bill, aimed at curtailing the efforts of tabloid newspapers to reveal people's private lives. Murdoch confessed: 'I fiddled with that one a bit'.

In that case *The Sun* said:

The Establishment does not like The Sun. Never has.

We are so popular they fear our success, since they do not understand the ordinary working man and woman.

The Sun has never much worried about the views of the Establishment. Until now.

Now we are concerned.

Because there is a growing band of people in positions of influence and privilege who want OUR newspaper to suit THEIR private convenience. They wish to conceal from the

readers' eyes anything that they find annoying or embarrassing to themselves.

Living lies and hypocrisy on high can have no place in our society.

If a star who profits enormously by being idolised takes drugs we shall say so. Such an act is a public breach of trust.

If a TV performer who sets himself up as a paragon of domestic decencies is a lying sham, we shall say so.'

When politicians supposedly serving the public are on the private make, we shall tell our readers.

So what about The Sun? Do we make mistakes? Of course we do. Sometimes they are our own fault. Sometimes we are deceived by liars and phoneys.

And by God do we pay for them.

Our readers want us to be questioning, courageous and free. The 'privacy' lobby would prefer tame, timid newspapers that are as much the house magazine of the Establishment as Pravda is the parrot voice of the Kremlin.

For The Sun's part we shall fight to stay exactly as we are.

It is not just our struggle.

It is the struggle of all those concerned for freedom in Britain.

But Rupert Murdoch had no hand at all in one recent leader which sent shock waves half way round the world.

It was headed 'HELL'S WAITING FOR THIS TRULY EVIL EMPEROR' and was an unfond farewell to the dying Emperor Hirohito of Japan. It began:

> There are two reasons for sadness as Emperor Hirohito lies on his deathbed.
>
> The FIRST is that he lived as long as he did.
>
> The SECOND is that he died unpunished for some of the foulest crimes of this violent century.

It wound up:

> At the end, did he suffer any of the pain or sorrow of his

multitude of victims?

We shall never know.

But when he goes, he will surely be guaranteed a special place in Hell.

'That was very much Kelvin,' says Rupert Murdoch, referring to *Sun* editor MacKenzie. 'Sometimes he doesn't talk to me at all.'

That editorial resulted in a strong letter of protest from the Japanese Embassy in London. In Tokyo, the British Ambassador was called to the Japanese Foreign Ministry to receive an official protest.

Murdoch describes his first reactions: 'I thought, you shouldn't do this; this is embarrassing. But then the report from the War Crimes Commission in Australia comes and you find that these people lived on human flesh.'

By and large, *The Sun* does not like foreigners.

When Spanish air traffic controllers went on strike, *The Sun* said, 'If you don't like your job, Señor, why don't you quit and take up bull-fighting, bird strangling or donkey torturing?'

When French farmers tried to stop British lamb arriving in their country, *The Sun* urged its readers:

> *If you are a housewife doing the weekend shopping today, do not buy a single item of French produce, nothing from camembert to their rotten golden delicious apples.*
>
> *If you want wine, choose German, Italian, Spanish, even Chateau Dorking.*
>
> *Nothing – not even l'amour – is as close to a Frenchman's heart as his wallet.*
>
> *Let's hit him there and go on hitting him until he stops behaving like some evil robber baron out of the darkest pages of history.*

On the subject of Japanese trade practices, *The Sun* urged: 'Mrs Thatcher saw off the Argies. She must now see off the Japs.'

And despite the Down Under origins of *The Sun*'s owner, it has also bashed the Australians:

Pommie-bashing is an old Australian pastime.

But once it was based on affection and friendship. Today it springs from malice.

Maybe it is time we started being frank about the Land of Oz.

It used to be called the lucky country because it possessed vast resources and hard-living people.

Today it is an almighty mess.

Its trade unions are dominated by Marxist wreckers. Beer-bellied workers prefer the beach to the factory.

Its cricketers are pathetic.

Of its recent premiers[sic], Whitlam tried to destroy the constitution. Malcolm Fraser lost his trousers on an American speaking tour. And the present luminary, Bob Hawke, is given to tears in moments of stress.

Britain has nothing – but nothing – to learn from the new cobbers.

All they are good at is whingeing!

Since the early days of *The Sun*, the language of the leaders has become more direct – and certainly more vicious.

Ronald Spark says that is just a sign of the times: 'If you listen to an argument in a pub it tends to get a bit over-heated. Things are said in a more direct way nowadays and I don't see any harm in that.'

For instance, when Iran's Ayatollah Khomeini threatened to kill British author Salman Rushdie, *The Sun* advised action from the prime minister: 'She must warn the vile old swine that he personally will pay for any attack on Rushdie.'

'Make sure your mouth and brain are connected.' it advised Sir John Harvey-Jones, chairman of ICI, who criticized the way *Sun* printers were treated over the newspaper's move to its high-tech headquarters in Wapping. The writer added that Sir John 'appears to have gone off his double-barrelled rocker'.

There was short shrift for actor Leslie Grantham after he attacked newspapers in a radio interview. 'If brains were made of elastic, actor Leslie Grantham would not have enough to make a knee support for a one-legged sparrow.'

And a lot of readers must have winced when Spark wrote: 'Neil Kinnock obviously believes the public's memory is as short as a retarded dwarf'.

But *Sun* leaders have fans in high places. A Foreign Office circular sent to embassies a while ago told them to try to write their reports like *Sun* leaders.

Sir Keith Joseph once said in the House of Commons, during the first half of *The Sun*'s life when editorials were regularly on the paper's second page: 'Page two of *The Sun*, the editorial page, is a very valuable page for the country.'

Sir William Rees-Mogg, former editor of *The Times* and now head of the Broadcasting Standards Council, says, 'I have an almost unlimited admiration for *Sun* leaders, which I think are among the finest expressions of current British popular journalism. They are punchy, pithy, interesting and easy to read.'

Not everyone admires them, though. Writer Spark was suspended from the National Union of Journalists for his efforts during the Falklands War when he accused TV commentator Peter Snow of treason for questioning the government's version of events. And he was later expelled after praising a Derbyshire council which decided not to employ gays in jobs dealing with children.

The one section of the community which virtually must start the day by digesting what 'The Sun Says' is the House of Commons. The prime minister would not turn up for work without doing so and it would be unwise for any MP not to be informed in the same way.

What 'The Sun Says' on page six (sometimes page one or page two) is a fair guide to what 12 million people are thinking.

And for those who don't read editorials there is *The Sun*'s cartoonist, Franklin, who also gets the paper's message across with a punch that would make Frank Bruno proud.

Franklin is said to have earned Neil Kinnock's hatred with such efforts as his cartoon of Kinnock meeting Reagan. Or his front-page cartoon where Kinnock is held down by a huge Russian solider's boot as he waves a catapult.

When Jim Callaghan was prime minister, Franklin took to drawing him as Mr Micawber in the lead up to the 1979 election. 'I had been attacking him for about eighteen months before I was summoned to meet him during a Labour party conference in Blackpool,' Franklin recalls. 'He said, "So you're the cartoonist who is always attacking me."

'I said, "Yes, but it is the prerogative of the press to criticize the prime minister."' To which he replied, "I know, Mr Franklin, but every day?"'

One of the political characters Franklin says he most enjoyed drawing was former Labour leader Michael Foot: 'In one cartoon, I drew him very small and he looked marvellous as a dwarf so I drew him like that from then on.

'A friend once told me his old mother had seen Foot being interviewed on telly and called out, "Come and look at this! There's someone on TV that looks like one of Franklin's characters."'

Plenty of Franklin's victims ask for the original of the cartoon depicting themselves. Major Ronald Ferguson was so tickled by one referring to his indiscreet visits to a massage parlour that he wrote asking for it. The poor man then had to suffer his request being turned into a front-page story. But the framed work of art was later sent to him at the Guards Polo Club at Windsor.

Michael Heseltine also requested the original of a cartoon showing him making his exit from the Cabinet at the time of the Westland helicopter row.

And Clint Eastwood asked for Franklin's picture comment when he was standing for mayor of Carmel, California. He was shown threatening voters with the ultimate punishment for not electing him: the noose. It was a reproduction of a famous scene from an Eastwood film, *Hang Them High*, and had obviously made the star's day.

Prince Charles has the original of a Franklin cartoon published just after the revelation by Archbishop Runcie that he had advised the prince and his new bride on sex. The caption was 'Charles thinks His Grace's collar should be worn higher'. The picture shows him wearing it round his mouth.

" CHARLES THINKS HIS GRACE'S COLLAR SHOULD BE WORN HIGHER!"

But the Duchess of York has *not* got the original of the cartoon showing an enormous pair of her knickers being auctioned at Christies. The auctioneers themselves put in for that one.

4. Call That a Newspaper?

The news desk at *The Sun* is banked with telephones and computer screens scrolling up the day's news as it comes in from sources throughout Britain and abroad.

On the wall behind are a trio of flying brown rabbits and a flight of plaster penguins – replacements for the flying ducks which were stolen one weekend and became the subject of a 10 pound ransom demand.

A multi-coloured fluffy parrot hangs above the desk – the ideal pet, as news editor Tom Petrie explains: 'A real parrot would have heard nothing but bad language all day. We couldn't have let anyone take it home on their holidays because it might have upset their granny. All we do with this one is put it in a washing machine once a year.'

There is also what is known as the True Story Alert. This is a rubber spitting image of Mrs Thatcher that squawks when squeezed. It got its role one day when a young showbiz reporter, famous for his dodgy news tip-offs, came to the desk with yet another of his suspect scoops. He wound up his outline of the story by shouting, 'AND IT'S TRUE!'

Editor Kelvin MacKenzie, standing nearby, grabbed the squeaky toy, using it to announce, 'True story alert, folks, we have a true story here.' It became the news desk joke, every time there were doubts about a story's accuracy.

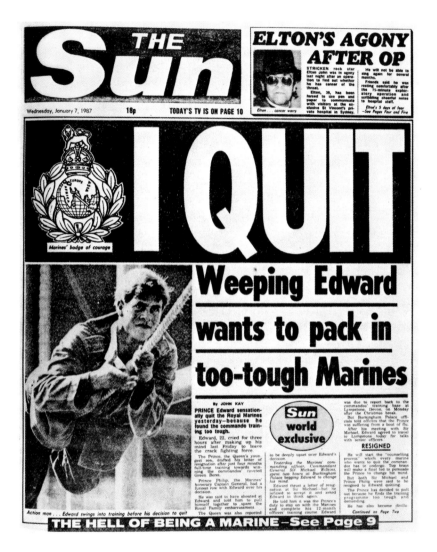

announcement that Prince Edward was quitting because of a leg injury.'

That is the version that would have gone down in history but for the *The Sun*. Reporter Kay managed to get categorical confirmation that Prince Edward was going to resign and put it to the Queen's then press secretary Michael Shea.

'I have no information to give you,' was the official word from the Palace.

When that night's first edition hit the streets, all *The Sun*'s rivals were forced to pick up the story. And next day the Palace officially confirmed that Edward was considering his future as a marine.

The day after that, another *Sun* exclusive told how Edward would have to buy his way out of the marines. He eventually did so for just over £10,000.

Intensive investigations by the police, the Ministry of Defence and the marines failed to uncover the source of *The Sun* story.

Another great *Sun* royal scoop was the naming of the Duke and Duchess of York's first baby four days before the official announcement from Buckingham Palace.

It was the biggest guessing game in the press in August 1988 and bookies were taking bets – but one name never mentioned was Beatrice.

Reporter John Kay once again got 'inside information': the baby was to be christened Beatrice Elizabeth Mary.

Everyone in *The Sun* office expressed astonishment – and disbelief. No one could believe it was a 'proper' royal name. But the clinching factor was Kay's discovery that Queen Victoria had named one of her daughters Beatrice.

Kay, a betting man, says you would have got 500-1 at the bookies with a bet on 'Beatrice'. But no one at *The Sun* got the chance. The bookies had stopped taking bets because they feared there might be a betting coup.

This may have had something to do with the fact that, just before Prince William's name was announced, a £500 bet on the name was placed at a betting shop not a million miles from Buckingham Palace.

On the day *The Sun* announced the names of Fergie's baby there was complete silence from Buckingham Palace which then waited four days before confirming that the child was indeed to be called Beatrice Elizabeth Mary.

Yet again a police investigation into the leak failed to reach its source.

Those stories were the result of chance tip-offs. But most of *The Sun*'s royal stories come from the reporters who regularly follow members of the royal family around – not only on royal tours but on day-to-day engagements.

This concentration on the royals started in earnest when Prince Charles came out of the navy. He was twenty-eight and had once expressed the view that thirty was a good age for a man to marry. *The Sun*'s editor of the time, Larry Lamb, was determined *The Sun* would win the race to announce that Charles had met his match. He appointed the paper's first permanent royal roundsmen. Their brief: to follow the prince on a daily basis.

That is how *Sun* writer Harry Arnold and photographer Arthur Edwards came to the very early conclusion that Lady Diana Spencer might become the future queen of England.

What this means is that the royal reporters have been able to build up an amazing network of contacts and 'moles' over the years. Royal estate workers, footmen, detectives, they all pass on the tit-bits of information that enable reporters to work out what's going on behind palace walls.

Take Fergie's pregnancy. *The Sun*'s star royal photographer Arthur Edwards was told by a Sandringham estate worker that the Duchess of York had been heard to say: 'Can't stay. Got to go and rest. Doctor's orders.' Just afterwards, Arthur and royal writer Harry Arnold saw Fergie in Switzerland and, fathers both, spotted the sure signs of morning sickness.

'We broke the story', says Arthur. 'And then we spent ten days on tenderhooks till Buckingham Palace finally announced it.'

'I was at Cowdray Park Polo Club in July 1980 when a good contact of mine told me that Prince Charles and Lady Diana Spencer were staying with the prince's old friend, Commander Robert de Pass,' Arthur recalls. 'We spotted her with a group of friends in the private members' enclosure next to the clubhouse.'

The girl they saw was wearing an open-necked blouse and flimsy skirt. Round her neck was a gold chain with the gold initial 'D' dangling from it.

The news-making photo: Lady Diana at Cowdray

He and Harry were only mildly interested. They noted that there seemed to be no contact at all between the prince and the girl he had brought to the polo. And when they checked and found that Diana was only eighteen, they were even less inclined to think there was anything in the relationship.

'I took a picture of her looking at me,' Arthur tells. 'Then I just told the library to file it.'

Two months later, at Balmoral for the Braemar Games, Arthur spotted Prince Charles with a girl on the riverbank. 'Straight away, she hid behind a tree, so I went and asked a Braemar contact who she

was. The reply was: "It's Lady Diana Spencer and she's following him round like a lamb."'

Harry filed a story, accompanied by the portrait of Diana plucked from *The Sun* library, under the headline 'He's in love again'.

The *Star* also ran a story, simply reporting that Prince Charles had been fishing with 'a pretty girl'.

It was a right royal scoop for *The Sun*, the first news, in September 1980, of the royal romance of the decade.

Those are some of the big royal stories. But there have been loads of small ones, at which *The Sun* excels. Who would have thought, for instance, that the heir to the throne's thinning hair would make the front page? That is exactly what happened when Arthur spied the beginnings of a bald patch on the back of Prince Charles' head and took two snaps of it. 'Oops Charles There's a Patch in Your Thatch' was the headline.

A patch in his thatch . . .

It was one of Edwards' first picture-stories about the prince and he was anxious not to offend His Royal Highness, so asked for his by-line to be left off the picture.

Too late. Arthur's name appeared and three days later he was approached by one of the prince's detectives who said, 'He'd like a word with you.'

'Are you the one who photographed the back of my head?' the prince demanded, adding: 'Fortunately not too many people saw it.'

'Only about 12 million,' Edwards informed him, then asked, 'Why, sir, have you been taking some stick over it?'

'No,' said the prince. 'But everyone keeps photographing the back of my head.' Then, looking at Edwards' own receding hairline, he said, 'You're not doing too brilliantly yourself.'

'No,' Arthur admitted, 'but I'm eight years older than you.'

There have been many exchanges since between the two, most of them friendly, many of them funny.

In December 1988 the royal family were under a lot of fire from the press. And when the prince spotted Arthur at Sandringham just before Christmas he started to complain about being pestered by photographers.

Arthur said, 'Prince Charles only reads the *Guardian* so I told him, "Your family has been getting a lot of stick in *The Sun*".

He said, "I don't read it, Mr. Edwards, and I hope you don't either."

The prince does not know what he's missing. He may not like the paper's royal coverage but there are a lot of other stories with what news editor Petrie feels are essential ingredients to tickle the palates of *Sun* readers – a sense of fun and the capacity to amaze.

Petrie cites an example: 'We ran a story about a couple who had won £40,000-odd at bingo. They only had one child and they blew the lot on microwaves, televisions, videos and such, then went back to the DHSS for a handout.

'The day the story appeared I was visiting my son. There were five people in the house and I watched as each one read the paper at different times. They ALL stopped when they got to that story and said, "Crikey, look at that."

'That sort of story is compulsive reading and it is the lifeblood of *The Sun*.'

Big disasters like air and train crashes occupy many pages of *The Sun*, which will devote most of an issue to a major story. 'I'd be prepared to bet we give more space to big stories than our rivals. I think big stories are easy,' says Tom Petrie. 'You just have to make sure you get it ALL.'

That is why armies of *Sun* news reporters and photographers turn up whenever there is a major catastrophe. Some might call it overkill – to Petrie it is just covering all the options.

A high point in the paper's popularity was reached during the Falklands War when *The Sun* gave itself the title 'The Paper That Supports Our Boys.' Headlines like 'GOTCHA' (when the *Belgrano* was hit) and 'UP YOURS GALTIERI' were not to everyone's taste but they obviously caught the mood of the moment.

'We now regard ourselves as the Forces' paper, which the *Mirror* used to be,' Petrie says, 'We get lots of Forces stories in the paper and great feedback from them.'

The Sun has been accused of being jingoistic and its Falklands coverage obviously stirred its readers' patriotic feelings. It's arrival among our boys at war was not always greeted with pleasure, however. A young officer wounded in the hostilities told a *Sun* journalist afterwards: 'Your headlines often made us feel sick. There were ritual burnings of *The Sun* in some quarters.'

The Sun's Tony Snow was the reporter covering the war. He's never forgotten moments like the landings in San Carlos Bay, for which he was transferred from the *Invincible* to an ammunition ship full of missiles and eighty fed-up marines.

'We were in the middle of Bomb Alley and we knew we could go up like a rocket if we got hit – yet suddenly we were told NOT to observe the strict regime we'd got used to on *Invincible*, to put away the full-length rubber suits we wore, the gas masks, the life jackets and anti-flash gear.

'The captain told us to leave all that stuff in our cabins – because it upset the marines. He said they didn't like to be reminded of the fact that people on other ships had a chance of survival if they got hit.

'When I asked what would happen if we got hit, he said, "Put it this way: you won't need a lifeboat, you'll need a parachute."

'The poor marines were really sick at the thought they could be blown away without lifting a finger to defend themselves.'

There were lighter moments for *The Sun*'s man at war. A practical fellow, Tony knew just how to fill the empty hours when newsmen aboard *Invincible* were instructed: 'You can do a story this morning but then you can do nothing for another six hours because there will be an attack going on.'

In the cabin he shared with four others, he got out his notebook and a yellow expenses claim form on which he began to type out claims for money he had spent before being sent to war.

'The captain's assistant came in and said, "I thought I told you – NO MORE STORIES." He was a bit jittery because the Argies kept aiming at *Invincible*. So I said, "It's not a story, I'm catching up on my expenses."

'The other lads were laughing but he exploded, "Expenses! At a time like this!"

'That night in the bar somebody said to me there was a nasty rumour that at the height of the day's attack I'd been doing my exes.

'The story had gone round the ship: 'There's nothing to worry about, folks. The bloke from *The Sun* is doing his expenses.'

Everyone likes a laugh on *The Sun*. Other newsmen also long to know what *The Sun* is up to.

This was one of those rare occasions when they did not have to worry.

5. Give Enough Monkeys Enough Cameras

Photographers are known in Fleet Street as monkeys. Appropriately, *The Sun* snappers held their last Christmas party at London Zoo. They are the sort to see the funny side – and in their job it is just as well.

Every picture tells a story, they say. But often that story is nothing compared to the one about how the picture was obtained. Taking pictures the subjects do not want taken has become the name of the game in tabloid journalism where the snatched picture usually has more news value than the set-up one.

It can, of course, get the snapper into trouble. But as any of them will tell you, that only gives the job extra excitement. Photographers' tales are in the same league as big game hunters' and fishermen's.

One of *The Sun*'s best (worst?) escapades was the snatched picture of a very pregnant Princess of Wales in a bikini, taken on holiday in the West Indies before the birth of Prince William.

The picture itself was harmless enough – she looked like any other expectant young mother on a beach – but the Queen was highly unamused by it and protested about invasion of privacy. Whereon *The Sun* splashed one of the offending pictures on its front page the following day, alongside an editorial headed 'THE SUN THE QUEEN AND THOSE PICTURES . . .' which defended their use.

Arthur Edwards, the photographer who took the pictures, says:

'That was the most misery we ever caused the royals. We were sent to beat the *Star* and it was all quite a drama. Both of us got the pictures at the same time and rushed to wire them back to England. Competition was so strong that when I told the editor I was at that moment on the wire machine, he said, "When you finish with it, could you put an axe through it?" – anything to stop the *Star* getting their picture through.'

In the end, *The Sun* beat the *Star* by just one edition, due to a little dirty work by Edwards who gave two pictures to the agency whose machine he borrowed, on condition they did not let the *Star* use the machine.

He was a hero to his editor. But he admits feeling low as he returned to Britain knowing there were questions asked in Parliament over his escapade and that there was a lot of media criticism. He felt even worse when one of the office drivers who saw him arriving back spat on the ground and said, 'You guys are scum.'

The pictures were sold round the world, of course, which gave Arthur another bad moment the following year when he came face to face with the Princess of Wales at a press reception in Alice Springs, Australia.

'She told me, "I gather you made a lot of money out of those pictures." She didn't realize it was my employer who made the money, not me.

'I told her I got the same money whether I covered her in the Bahamas or a court case in Bradford.

'Her reply to that was, "Oh, pass me the Kleenex."'

There was more royal displeasure when *The Sun* splashed its ill-gotten snap of four generations of the royal family – baby Beatrice, the Duchess of York, the Queen and Queen Mother – all over its front page in late 1988. Charming picture. But *The Sun* had no right to use it as it was a picture 'stolen' from the laboratory where it had been sent by the Queen for reproduction on Her Majesty's private Christmas cards. So – more rapped knuckles for *The Sun*.

A picture taken by a freelance photographer was the evidence *The Sun* needed when it was hot on the trail of Prince Charles' romance with 'Lady Di'. That little snap of Diana's car parked in the yard at Buckingham Palace told the paper's royal team that the engagement was imminent. It appeared under the headline 'DI GOES TO THE PALACE'.

Other winning royal pictures were chance snaps taken at moments when photographers were not expected to be present. The Princess of Wales in her tennis whites at the Vanderbilt Club was one. Another

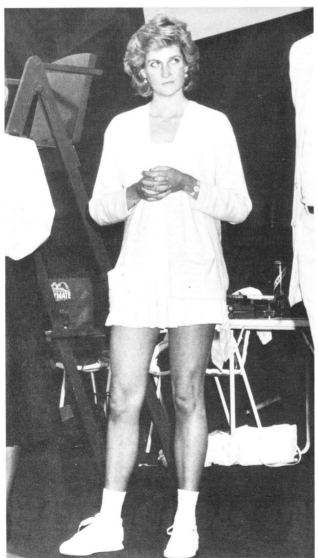

© Press Association

was a sneaked snap of her dancing with Wayne Sleep at a Friends of Covent Garden charity performance.

Sun picture editor Paul Buttle says picture styles have changed a lot in the nine years since he took on the job. And they have changed dramatically since the first days of the paper when the photographs that had people talking were the dramatic portrait of Britain's last hangman, Albert Pierrepoint, or the sitting-room study of Sir Matt Busby with his three children, taken to illustrate a feature about love.

There is more of a spontaneous element in today's pictures, which are likely to have been taken on the hop by a photographer often as surprised as his subject. Thus Arthur Edwards, sent to Klosters, Switzerland, on the off-chance of a picture of Prince Charles' injured skiing friend, Patti Palmer-Tompkinson, returned with one of the rarest images of all: a snap of hideaway screen queen, Greta Garbo.

Recluse Greta Garbo – an unexpected coup for Arthur Edwards

And Steve Lewis, dejected over a failed feature assignment in Ibize, managed to recover from it tenfold when he chanced on the sort of picture photographers dream about – actress Julie Goodyear, Bet Lynch from 'Coronation Street', cheerfully topless, sipping tropical cocktails with a young male companion on the beach.

It's not a situation where you ask permission. Lewis quietly parked himself in the sand dunes, got his cameras ready and waited for the couple to walk up the beach towards him. At the last minute he leaped up and snapped. Lewis then had to leg it over the sands pursued by three burly defenders of Julie's privacy who then laid seige to the photographer's hotel.

'All I knew was, I had to get off the island with the pictures,' he says. So, with help from the hotel manager early the next day, he sprinted through a back door to his hired car and sped to an airport getaway.

Another star Lewis caught on holiday was Samantha Fox, whom he followed to Kenya where she and a boyfriend were preparing for a secret safari.

When he confronted them in Nairobi, they agreed to do some pictures during a four-day safari tour, provided he would then disappear. What they didn't tell Lewis was that the trip finished in a godforsaken village 400 miles from Nairobi – and there was no room for him on the chartered plane back.

'It was their revenge. I was standing on this tiny runway when they took off and Sam was falling about laughing – as she took a picture of me. I had to do a deal with the pilot to come back again.'

Samantha Fox's photo call that ended in revenge

Jim Davidson proved a difficult customer when Lewis tracked him down on honeymoon in Barbados – even though, as Lewis puts its, 'I've photographed him with all his wives and gone on all his honeymoons.'

'He wouldn't do anything till he had an agreement with the editor to pay him a suitable fee. At one point he was walking up and down the beach with a mobile phone trying to up the ante with Kelvin in London.'

'Finally we did the pictures and at the very end Davidson said, ''Hey, this one's for Kelvin,'' and dropped his trousers.'

Lewis got that one back to London and when editor Kelvin MacKenzie spied it, that was the shot to appear in the paper, under the headline – 'NICK-NICKERLESS.'

It appeared yet again in the paper six days later, headed – 'Jim's Missus May Get Bum's Rush.' The story was that Davidson's wife, HTV newsreader Alison Holloway, was in trouble with her bosses over the picture.

Veteran photographer Arthur Steel was one of only three of the world's top press photographers to snap the Prince and Princess of Wales' famous wedding-day kiss on the balcony at Buckingham Palace. He was among 150 of them on a special stand on the roundabout outside the Palace when it happened. Luckily he was focused on the happy couple, unlike others who were re-loading cameras or distracted by the sudden appearance of the princess's parents on the balcony.

'I was next to David Bailey who missed it,' says Steel, whose picture was on the front page of nearly every national daily the next day. He was 'rota man' which meant he was representing not only *The Sun* at the time but all of Fleet Street.

Another Steel exclusive was a picture of Harold Wilson and his wife, Mary, asleep on each other's shoulders in the back of their car after he had lost the 1970 election. He recalls: 'I had cadged a lift back from Wilson's constituency in Huyton, Liverpool, with the man from the *Daily Express*. The Wilsons were driving in a big convoy back to Ten Downing Street where they had to hand over to Edward Heath. I spotted their heads nestling together and said, "Let's go for it."'

The most famous scoop of all

'We pulled out and overtook the car, each getting one chance at the picture. I was lucky but the *Express* man got all the window bars.'

They were severely reprimanded by police for their pains, for causing a security scare. Steel was also ticked off for another Wilson chance picture, when he spied Mary Wilson making notes at a Labour party Common Market conference. He was in a gallery above where she sat, so he took a 'spy' picture with a long lens. The notes turned out to be a shopping list for bread, butter and sugar and the picture earned Steel a threatened ban from the next Labour party conference.

He was in worse trouble when police actually arrested him one day as he photographed a model – clothed – hugging armfuls of daffodils in London's Hyde Park. A Park Lane resident had spotted him from an upstairs window and thought he had picked the daffs in the park.

Arthur had in fact bought them from a barrow in a nearby side street. Nevertheless, the police still tried matching up the stalks of his flowers to some broken stems they found in the park.They did not let him go till he led them to the barrow where he had bought them.

However, he got one past the police when he was snapping a series of pictures of 'Beautiful Britain', taking models round the country's beauty spots. He did not realize, till he got there, that Stonehenge was surrounded by trip-wires linked to an underground police station beneath the famous stones. And he had planned to photograph a nude girl there very early in the morning.

'We had to wait to pay to go in with the other visitors. The girl was wearing just her coat and as soon as no one was looking, she whipped it off, sat down among the spring flowers and we did the picture.'

Imagination paid off when Robert Runcie was named Archbishop of Canterbury in 1979. Steel noted that tennis was listed among his hobbies so he rang and asked if he could photograph His Grace on the court. The result: a set of very funny pictures of Britain's leading churchman.

Steel was inspired again one wet day at Wimbledon when rain not only stopped play for the day but flooded the courts. It was a dismal sight. No players, no crowds, no picture? If only a couple of ducks would pop by for a paddle in the water, thought Steel. Then he thought, Why don't I just nip to a shop and buy some plastic ones?

That done, he went to an outside court so as not to be spotted by some of his colleagues still trying for their wet day picture. Out came the ducks from under his coat, into the water they went and, snap, Arthur had his picture. Quickly he snatched them up and stuffed them in his pockets. But unknown to him he was being watched by colleagues who could see him on closed circuit television in the press bar.

Steel says, 'Next thing you know, half of Fleet Street was off down to the shops for plastic ducks. Within minutes you couldn't buy a toy duck in the whole of Wimbledon.'

6. Who Reads It?

How do you make a *Sun* reader burn his ear? Answer: Phone him when he's ironing his trousers.

Ouch! Comedian Jasper Carrott had audiences in stitches with his '*Sun* reader' jokes. He even used to claim it was OK to offend *Sun* readers because they couldn't write in to complain.

He was wrong about that: *The Sun* postbag was stuffed with letters from angry readers pointing out that they could not only read and write, they could also switch off the BBC late on Saturday nights.

The one thing you can always guarantee with *Sun* readers, they respond. If there is a story that upsets or offends them, a picture they find tasteless or distressing, a factual error or a minor misprint, they send in angry letters by the avalanche.

They also phone. And sometimes they get the ear of the last person they expect on the other end: the editor.

Kelvin MacKenzie, who has edited *The Sun* since 1981, is a one-man swarm. Not the kind of editor who stays in his office and lets staff come to him, he roams constantly round the editorial floor sticking his nose into everything going on. And if he is standing near a phone that rings, he will almost always pick it up.

That was how he came to receive an earful one day from a very angry reader who disagreed vehemently with something *The Sun* had just published and who finished his tirade by saying, 'And I'm never going to buy your paper again.'

'What's your name? Who's your newsagent?' asked MacKenzie. The man told him.

MacKenzie then roared, 'From now on, you are BANNED from buying *The Sun*.' Then he hung up.

The next day a woman rang the news desk with a query: 'Er, yesterday you banned my husband from buying your paper. Does that mean I can't get it either?'

'You can,' she was told. 'As long as you don't let your old man see it. But if we hear he's been having a look, we'll have to ban you too.' The woman rang off, sounding puzzled.

But you could not be *sure* who was winding up whom.

Sun readers are far from stupid. Despite the jokes, it is a fact that *The Sun* is read by more of the professional and technically skilled members of the community than any other daily newspaper. These are members of the AB and C1 groups, as defined by the advertising industry. ABs are highly qualified professionals like doctors, lawyers, architects, MPs; C1s include college lecturers, teachers, computer programmers, draughtsmen. A quarter of *The Sun'* readers – about 3 million – are in this bracket.

This is more AB and C1 readers than read the country's top-selling 'quality' newspaper, the *Daily Telegraph*. Therefore more top people read *The Sun* than read *The Times*, the *Guardian* or the *Independent*. So there. Perhaps all *The Sun*'s secret readers, the ones who say they've never bought it but you can't escape it at work, in the train, at the hairdresser, the barber . . . can take heart and own up.

The paper's readership is also young: 46 per cent are in the fifteen to thirty-four age group. And 48 per cent of the readers are women – so much for the view that Page Three is what sells the paper. (Perhaps it is the Page Seven Fella, the bare-chested hunk who appears once a week to give the girls a thrill?)

For just over 6 million adults in Britain, *The Sun* is their only daily newspaper. And readers are very loyal. More than half the adults surveyed in 1988 who say they had read *The Sun* in the past year had read at least three out of four issues. Just over one-third said the same of the *Daily Mirror, Daily Express, Daily Mail* and *Star*.

The hapless headmaster of a school in Burton-on-Trent sent a circular letter to the parents of all his pupils in 1982 after a student told *The Sun* she had been banned from the school's Christmas party for wearing green socks.

The head told parents, 'One of our girls got her picture in *The Sun*. I'd better tell you I was a bit shocked to find so many of our children see *The Sun* for I thought none of our mothers would have it in the house.

'It's no good our teaching people to read if they then go home and read rubbish.'

Up-in-arms mothers all responded by phoning *The Sun*. The paper then ran an editorial accusing the head of insulting its 12 million readers and hitting back: 'We are also concerned for his pupils when he can write "one of our girls GOT her picture in *The Sun*" and imagine that is English.'

It also published a letter from a trucker called Dave who claimed he had learned to read as an adult by studying *The Sun*. And another letter from nine undergraduates at St Peter's College, Oxford University, who all praised *The Sun* as the most popular paper in their junior common room.

Nobody sees *The Sun*'s great cross-section of readers quite like the people at the receiving end of the thousands of letters that arrive at the paper's Wapping office each week. Letters Page editor Sue Cook has to deal with 2500 to 3000 letters a week and agony aunt Deidre Sanders replies to 1100 a week on average – though her biggest week totalled nearly 5000.

That probably answers that niggling thought, on reading a letter from a mother of six whose husband likes dressing up as a bridesmaid to have sex, that all those letters must be made up.

'I *couldn't* make up some of the questions readers ask,' says Deidre, who is spoiled for choice when it comes to selecting letters to publish. Far from spicing them up to entertain readers, she frequently has to tone them down. My problem is not to find exciting enough letters, but to find ones that will interest a wide range of readers, be frank, but not too shocking.'

She is often surprised by the subjects that cause sudden interest – like small boys wearing short trousers. Deidre was swamped with letters, supposedly from little lads, when she tried to advise a widower father on whether or not his thirteen-year-old son should switch to the long trousers he badly wanted. It suddenly dawned that most of her letters were from middle-aged men, among whom there is a certain short-trouser cult.

All letters seeking help from Deidre receive personal replies, a fact which caused a brief skirmish with editor MacKenzie who arrived about a year after she replaced her predecessor, the formidable Claire Rayner.

Anxious about the enormous cost of answering Deidre's mail, he wondered if it was strictly necessary? She argued that no one would write if they thought there was little chance of an answer.

Shortly after this heated argument, the box attached to her column telling people how to write sending a stamped addressed envelope for reply disappeared.

That day in the column was a letter from a reader thanking Deidre for her help – she had just had her first orgasm in sixteen years of marriage after studying a leaflet on the subject compiled by Deidre. Deidre then offered the leaflet to anyone who wished to write for it.

Because the usual specific address for Deidre was missing, the 10,000 readers wanting the orgasm leaflet wrote to the first address they could find in the paper – which happened to be the one for bingo entries.

The first anyone knew about it was a week later, when Deidre started getting letters from confused readers saying, 'I wrote off for an orgasm leaflet and got back a bingo-card – what am I meant to do?'

Deidre's postal address has appeared ever since. And what used to be her weekly column now appears daily, on the instruction of boss Rupert Murdoch.

Time and again it comes home to Deidre that her job is actually saving lives, in many cases filling holes in the safety net of the welfare state.

Take the case of the young single mother who wrote that she loved her seven-week-old baby very much but could not cope. She had gone out and left the baby – who seemed lifeless and wasn't eating much – at home. The mother thought her baby might be dying and that the only solution was to kill both of them. The letter was anonymous but bore a South London postmark.

Deidre says, 'I couldn't get the letter in the paper for a week, so I contacted the NSPCC who started checking hospital records in that area. I also contacted Parents Anonymous and alerted them to be prepared for the next Monday when I gave their number in the column for the girl to ring.

'We were all keyed up wondering what was going to happen, whether we would make contact with the girl. I wished and wished she had given me an address.

'However, at five o'clock that day, she did phone Parents Anonymous. And they ended up taking her baby to hospital. They were safe. Staff there said that considering the terrible post-natal depression she was suffering from, she had coped remarkably well.

'What I was not prepared for was that same day Parents Anonymous had heard from another fifty mothers, some in a much worse state than that girl, who had all seen the number in the paper. One had actually half-strangled her ten-year-old son.'

As well as the serious, sometimes even tragic letters that make up the bulk of Deidre's mail, there are the funnies that give the agony aunt a few moments' break from agony.

An elderly lady wrote that she and her seventy-five-year-old new lover were having a bit of trouble sexually. 'And yet he takes Sanatogen,' she explained.

One man who complained because his noisy neighbours disturbed him and his wife in bed at night added, 'Often it makes me lose my collection.' And a young man once wrote and complained of 'premature emancipation'.

A woman confessing to an almost accidental romance with her husband's best friend said, 'We had an affair but it wasn't international.' And a man who was upset because his wife spent her evenings picking up men at their local pub made Deidre grin when she noticed he lived in a place called Horfield.

Both Deidre and Letters Page editor Sue Cook say they are bowled over by their readers' generosity to each other. Any letter in the paper expressing need produces dozens of offers, from substantial cheques to gifts and job offers. Whenever a story of a hard-up family appears at Christmas-time in either column, hired vans are needed to disperse the gifts not only to that family but others in need as well.

When an elderly diabetic wrote to Sue that she could not afford a piece of equipment she needed, offers to buy it poured in – including one from Jimmy Savile.

Sun readers are encouraged to take part in nearly every area of the paper. They do it with gusto, from turning up in white studded jackets to enter an 'Are You The Real Elvis?' competition to saving coins to help sick children.

Take the case of the *Crying Boy*. There was a rumour that one of the only things left recognizable in a number of houses gutted by fire was a painting of a crying boy. It was a cheap picture, reproduced by the thousand and sold in places like market stalls and discount stores.

The Sun had the brilliant idea of wiping out the curse of the *Crying Boy*. Send us your pictures, it offered, and we will get rid of them forever. The idea was to burn them in the flames of a ceremonial bonfire. Pictures started arriving by the thousand. As a joke, someone hung one in the newsroom.

Editor MacKenzie did not see the funny side. 'What the bloody hell are you trying to do? Burn the place down?' he roared.

He obviously did not know about the ceiling-high mountain of *Crying Boys* stacked in a little-used interview room. This was where luckless journalists would have to spend the odd day receiving calls from *Sun* readers taking part in a phone-in survey.

As they picked up the phone with the words 'Sun Hotline', they fervently hoped it would not be.

7. Hold the Back Page

Vast numbers of *Sun* readers start the paper at the back. To them, the back page *is* the front page – which is why it is laid out to look exactly like it with familiar red *Sun* logo, big headlines, sensational stories and all.

This is the paper's sport section and its splashy presentation shows how important it is. In fact, when the sports writers talk about 'the front of the book' they mean the back.

The past twenty years has been a great era for sports journalists, a time when they stopped being referred to as 'the toy department' and came into their own. Television coverage, initially predicted to kill newspaper coverage of sporting events stone dead, has in fact pushed it into another league.

Senior *Sun* sportswriter Colin Hart, with the paper since its launch, says, 'The average person used to be not particularly interested in sport. But as television gave it more and more time, everyone became an expert – specially the women. They want to know all about people like snooker players.

'What people see on television they want to read about. TV and newspapers complement each other, they are not enemies.

'Television has upped the standards of sportswriting. You have to be more careful than ever to get the facts straight because people can see these events live on the box. Years ago people used to cheat and tell a few porkies to add colour to stories. But you can't do that any more because people can see for themselves.

'In the old days, you were reporting and describing events to tell people what they missed. Now you must give them the stories behind what they see on television.'

When 'Sunsport' was first envisaged, sports editor Frank Nicklin said it would have 'four rows of teeth'. He and his team overcame the enormous production difficulties to give it just that. Early deadlines meant that that day's sporting news stories were sometimes too late. So Nicklin concentrated on filling his pages with brilliant features.

Former editor, Bernard Shrimsley says, 'Frank was a master of the "nostalgia" feature. Not only was it not about last night, it was often not about last week – or even last year.' But the stories were good and the big names were always there.

'Sunsport' got off to a flying start. George Best, then on top of his form as one of the finest footballers ever, was signed up as a star columnist for *The Sun*'s launch.

The paper's football writer Frank Clough had to ghost-write the soccer star's articles. 'That crazy, mixed-up kid from Belfast will always be my all-time favourite player,' Clough says. 'He had the talent, the grace, the nerve, the instinct and the audacity to try for the impossible – and sometimes he achieved it.'

But as a newspaper contributor, Best was a nightmare. For Clough, his toughest job was not writing down Best's thoughts and views – it was finding him.

Birds, booze, nightclubs, gambling dens – these were Best's passions. When copy deadlines loomed, Clough was forever on the trail of Best's E-type Jaguar as the footballer chased a new girl, a new thrill.

Football coverage has always been one of *The Sun*'s great strengths. The paper was first with the news (on page one this time) that all-time England hero Bobby Charlton had decided to hang up his boots – on 16 April 1973.

They got it right ahead of the rest when they announced that

George Best – a Sun *columnist*

Manchester United was making a double bid of £2.5 million pounds in the autumn of 1981 for Bryan Robson and Remi Moses.

Terry Venables' switch from Queens Park Rangers to Barcelona made sport headlines in 1984 – another *Sun* first. And two years later the paper had a similar exclusive – headlined 'LINEKER YES TO EL TEL' – when it told how Barcelona had paid an amazing £2.5 million pounds for the services of Garry Lineker.

When Glen Hoddle, Spurs England ace, announced he was quitting Britain in December 1986 it was another scoop for 'Sunsport', as was Lawrie McMenemy's revelation in April 1987 that he would quit as Sunderland manager.

As a racing guide, *The Sun* has proved a winner all the way, not only for the quality of its tips but for the extent of its information.

'Tipster Templegate' made a brilliant start to a twenty-year career when he topped the National Hunt table in his first season – that is, his daily NAP selection was the most profitable among newspaper tipsters for the 1969-70 season.

This was the first of three Templegates, Lionel Cureton, who also topped the *Sporting Life* NAPs table in *The Sun's* first year. The second Templegate was John Hardie and the current one is Derek Mitchell – both have proved extra-profitable to the punters.

Three champion jockeys have also graced the paper's pages as racing columnists: Steve Cauthen and Willie Carson of flat racing, John Francome on the jumps.

The Sun is now indisputably the punters' paper, a role previously held by the *Daily Mirror* who in turn won it from the *Daily Express*.

A measure of *The Sun's* racing success is that Terry Clarke, racing editor since 1974, now has to fight off advertisers jockeying for space on his pages. 'All the bookmakers want to advertise with us,' he says.

The paper has continually updated and expanded its service to racing fans. In 1978 came the first *Sun Guide*, an annual pocket guide to the year's racing. It is now divided into two – *The Sun Guide to the Flat*, published each March, and *The Sun Guide to the Jumps*, published each November.

Then there are the 'Sunratings', a method of rating each horse by number in each race, the highest being 99. It is a simple, instant guide to the form and is so popular with punters that *The Times* has now copied it.

Roy Swan, the *Sun* racing writer who developed 'Sunratings', managed to produce forty winners with his first eighty-two selections.

But by far the greatest change in racing coverage has been 'Computercard', launched by *The Sun* in 1985 in time for the Grand National. This was the first time an English newspaper devoted a column to comparing the prices available for a race with each horse's real chance of winning.

Some bookmakers were quoting a horse called Last Suspect at 66-1. But 'Computercard' gave Last Suspect a 16-1 chance. When it romped home at 50-1, a new era in newspaper tipping began.

'Computercard' was not just experiencing beginners' luck, it proved its worth over and over till the time came when it became a necessity rather than a novelty. That was when an increasing number of races were being compiled during the morning of a race. What was known as 'the Morning Line' brought computer tipping into its own.

Race sponsorship was another way in which *The Sun* committed itself to the sport, along with its sister newspaper *News of the World*. Thus the Grand National was re-named the *News of the World* Grand National in 1975, 1976 and 1977 then re-christened *The Sun* Grand National in 1978, then 1980 to 1983.

History was made when Red Rum jumped to a record third victory in 'the greatest Chase on Earth' in 1977 – a sponsor's dream. It was also a first for News Group Newspapers that day, as sponsors of the whole day's racing. Apart from the main event, other races were run under *Sun* titles: the Sunratings Chase and The Templegate Hurdle.

By 1981, News Group's backing made *The Sun* Grand National the richest ever National Hunt race at £65,000. And this was only part of the whole day's prize-money which totalled £105,000.

1981 also produced a well-remembered result when old war-horse Aldaniti thundered home in the tender care of jockey Bob Champion, recently cured of cancer. That race became the climax of the film *Champions*.

Another great fighter who added colour and courage to the history of 'Sunsport' was the brilliant former heavyweight champion of the world Muhammad Ali. Boxing writer Colin Hart covered his fights for nearly twenty years and rates him as 'unquestionably the greatest sports personality of the century'.

Another great sports personality: Frank Bruno takes punishment dealt out by Tim Witherspoon, Wembley 1986

Along with sprinter Sebastian Coe, breaker of eleven world records and twice winner of Olympic gold, jockey Lester Piggot, winner of 4349 British races, twenty-nine of them classics, and footballer George Best, Ali has filled more newspaper columns than any other sports star.

Golden boy Sebastian Coe

Botham shares a refreshing lager with team-mate David Gower

These are the four sporting heroes who have dominated the past two decades – and they are still being written about.

As Hart points out: 'When Ali appeared at the Mike Tyson fight against Tyrell Biggs, the TV commentators forgot the fight and the cameras swivelled to focus on Ali as they speculated on the outcome of an Ali v. Tyson clash.'

But for the *Sun*'s boxing writer, the high point with Ali was what became known as 'the rumble in the jungle' - when Ali went to Zaire in 1974 to get his title back from George Foreman.

'When Ali made the daily trip from his training camp into the capital Kinshasa, the natives poured out in thousands to line the route and wave,' Hart remembers.

He also recalls the way things got sorted out when the world's sports writers were having difficulty getting their copy filed back to their sports desks.

'The telex operators there were so idle, you couldn't get a phone call out for three days. The operators used to hide and go to sleep. So we complained to their boss that it looked bad for the Zaire government.

'Next thing, President Mbutu put out an edict that the next telex operator found asleep on duty would be shot. They never stopped working after that.'

Since *The Sun*'s move to Wapping and its high-tech resources, the game has changed for the sports department. Bang up to the minute on results and sporting news, backed by excellent features, 'Sunsport' is almost a paper in itself. As today's sports editor David Balmforth says, 'We've got eight rows of teeth now.'

8. How To Sell a Lotto

On the office wall of *Sun* promotions director, Graham King, is a framed certificate from *The Guinness Book of Records* stating that the largest number of entrants in a newspaper competition was the 4,305,162 registered for the first *Sun* lotto game in March 1988.

What that meant was that for every copy of the paper sold, there was an entry in the competition – a 100 per cent entry rate. The norm is 2.5 per cent.

It was probably King's finest hour, the culmination of nearly twenty years of aggressively selling *The Sun*.

It all started with those set-your-teeth-on-edge, drive-you-nuts, throw-a-brick-at-the-box TV commercials which King developed and put on air in *The Sun*'s first year. Their slam-bang style was decidedly un-British, quite different from other newspaper commercials – and you could not fail to notice them.

They were fast and infuriating, packing in breathless information about the loads of goodies to expect in the paper that week: the stories, the competitions, the special offers, the amazing series. A rapid-fire voice-over delivered the words at 180-a-minute while a series of rivetting images flashed across the screen.

The star of these mini-spectaculars was an unknown actor from the Young Vic, chosen for his machine-gun delivery. He shot words out like bullets – except for one he never seemed to get his mouth around. Christopher Timothy, later to become famous as the star of the hit series, 'All Creatures Great and Small', could not say 'international'. It always came out 'internathonal'. Otherwise, he gave the magic touch to those early *Sun* commercials.

They looked amateurish and thrown-together and in a sense they were. 'Introducing the new technique was a bit of a culture shock for the advertising agency we used,' King admits.

This was magazine-concept advertising, filling the thirty- or sixty-second commercial with tempting details of the newspaper's contents. Other papers were then using generic advertising – projecting the personality and style of the product.

They were also only going on TV once the flat-racing season had started! King explains, 'There were all sorts of theories about rail points freezing up so you couldn't get the papers out. It seemed to be a rule that no one questioned.

'We decided to run a promotion before the flat. It worked so we did it earlier and earlier till we got right back to New Year. The *Daily Mirror* didn't wake up for two years to what was happening. Yet the effect of these new-style commercials was immediate and dramatic. You could count the increase in sales the day after they were shown.'

The *Sun* commercials were not always appreciated by the ITCA or the Independent Broadcasting Authority, however. Getting across the *Sun*'s saucy, sexy, lip-smacking, nudge-wink style inevitably involved clashes with the minders of TV viewers' morals.

Right at the start, there was a row over the commercial for Jacqueline Susann's *The Love Machine*. Every titillating idea was turned down till it was reduced to a visual of a man and a woman's hand sinuously moving together across a rumpled sheet.

A far worse rumpus came as a result of one commercial the ITCA let through, promoting a *Sun* series on 'The Sex Life of the Aristos'. It was at the time when 'Upstairs Downstairs' was the hottest thing on the box and King even got Jean Marsh, the actress who played the maid and who helped originate the series, to appear.

She played a housemaid making up a big four-poster in a stately home, gossiping about the goings-on in it. There was the usual battle but perhaps because Jean Marsh gave it credibility, it got through.

It did not, however, get past certain members of the aristocracy who noticed resemblances to themselves – and sued.

The most memorable commercial also, perhaps, deserved a *Guinness Book of Records* certificate – for the most complaints ever received about a commercial. It was for the *Sun* version of a book called *Rabid* which they tastefully retitled *The Day of the Mad Dogs*.

The scene: a middle-aged couple in their elegantly comfortable country sitting room, relaxing with their two dogs. Suddenly, the family pets leap up and start tearing at their owners, eyes wild, mouths frothing (thanks to a lather of shaving cream). A nightmare scene, followed by more and worse: screaming babies, terrified parents, hunters at night shooting down the savage beasts. And finally a dying victim, sweating out his last in a hospital bed.

The Sunday night commercial was taken off the air at about 11.00pm after the deluge of complaints.

But next morning *The Sun* literally walked off the newsagents' shelves.

But it is not only television that sells *The Sun*. Promotional offers have always played a big part in getting people to buy the paper.

These are bargains designed to be so irresistible that when you hear about them you want them. And to get them, you have to buy *The Sun*. Saucy black underwear has always been a winner – with both male and female customers. But you can't offer it every single week – even if it is packaged in tins, matchboxes, Christmas crackers or whatever.

So a team of people is fully employed looking for tempting new things to offer. And sometimes there is a catastrophe. Wigs, for instance.

They seemed like a brilliant idea at a time when they were a hot fashion gimmick. They were the right price and they looked stunning on *The Sun* models in the photographs.

But they apparently did nothing for the readers who ordered them in tens of thousands – and returned them in the same numbers. The offers department looked like a hay barn as bales of hair took over.

What was wrong with them was not the quality or the price. Readers just looked so funny in them that their husbands and boyfriends laughed and laughed. It went down as office lore that wigs are not a mail-order winner.

Roses were all set to be a selling success one winter. Readers sent off their cheques to order them by the field full. Unfortunately, the rose nursery was up north, the winter turned long and hard and the roses became frozen into the ground. They could not be dug out till late spring – so everyone demanded their money back.

Many *Sun* readers were on the *Herald of Free Enterprise* when it sank in Zeebrugge harbour in January 1987. It was the second year running that the paper had run trips to France for a pound-a-head as a special offer. It seemed macabre to repeat the offer in 1988.

Astoundingly, the offer was much more popular that year and again in 1989. A lot of people admitted they felt safer after the disaster – presumably on the grounds that it could not happen twice.

Bingo was one of the most successful promotions ever, specially as the idea was a direct steal from the *Daily Star. Sun* circulation reps in the north of England reported back that that paper was running a bingo game in a local edition and it seemed to be taking off in a big way *The Sun*, which had previously thought the game was not for newspapers, did a re-think.

Graham King went straight to Rupert Murdoch who said, 'Do it. Forget testing it – the *Star*'s done it for us. And do it nationally.'

So *Sun* bingo swept the country. And newspaper sales went up yet again.

'We've never tested anything,' is King's proud boast. 'We've never relied on research, it's always been seat of the pants, the test of the till.'

He is grateful, however, for one bit of research done by ARC, the company which makes *The Sun*'s commercials. They took a look at what the paper had in store for the 1990s on the basis of current trends. And this look at the future was disturbing: *The Sun*'s young readers were growing up, having their own children and there was nothing in the paper pulling in new young readers. All the promotions and serials appealed to older people. There hadn't been anything like a 'Pony Week' in the paper for twenty years.

'We needed to rejuvenate ourselves,' said King. And the answer to that turned out to be Lotto.

Bingo, it seems, is for the middle-aged and elderly. Its youth appeal is about zero. But lotto has something that bingo has not – choice. You choose your own numbers to play with, instead of being given them, as in bingo.

Enthusiasm for the game has been overwhelming, among both young and old. With 4.3 million playing lotto every day, who needs 'Pony Week'?

Of course, there are other prizes to be won in *The Sun* apart from money. The paper has given away most things in its time, from houses down to cans of beer.

But not all readers have been thrilled with their wins. There was a splendid villa in Tenerife won by a man who noticed that the house he won was slightly different from the one pictured in the paper. It was the shape of an archway that differed and when he questioned it, *The Sun* had to confess that its photographer had gone out there and snapped the wrong one. Otherwise, the house was all it was said to be: a fabulous villa on a sunshine island, if not *the* fabulous villa in the photo.

There was not a lot of sympathy in the promotions department when the winner tried to sue.

Another winner got more than he bargained for when he found himself the proud owner of a luxury bathroom – which did not fit into his small council house. However, he insisted it be installed, no matter that *The Sun* had virtually to rebuild his house.

And the paper's least successful competition was for twenty firkins of beer. Only thirteen entrants bothered to try for them.

9. Hey Girls!

Before the launch of the Murdoch *Sun,* women's pages in newspapers were full of fashion, beauty, babies, knitting patterns and recipes. *The Sun* called its women's pages 'Pacesetters' and filled them with sex.

They were produced *by* women *for* women. But they were sub-titled 'The pages for women that men can't resist', acknowledging that there are plenty of topics that fascinate both men and women. Like sex.

Who could resist an early series like 'The Geography of Love' – a run-down on where the best lovers in Britain were to be found? 'Do Men Still Want To Marry Virgins?' another feature asked. (The answer, in 1971, seemed to be: some do, most don't.) There was 'Love 30': women of that traumatic age talking about the facts of life and loving. 'I suppose you could say that I offer sympathy and sex. I never burden them with any of my troubles. One of my faults is that I'm not a good conversationalist. I find it much easier to express myself in bed,' admitted one fancy-free bachelor girl with four regular lovers. 'That First Night of Love' gave the rivetting details of that first-time experience for many women. Women readers were asked: 'Are You Getting Your Share?' Male readers were told how to find 'The Way into a Woman's Bed'. There was something for everyone in 'How To Be a Cool Lover' and again in 'How To Pick a Mate'.

A survey on sex and marriage in England in 1971 revealed that

'Despite all that talk of the "Permissive Society", the mass of English men and women do not pop into bed together. At least, not with just anyone.' The conclusion was that England was still 'a very chaste society' where nearly 90 per cent of women and 25 per cent of men claimed to have walked down the aisle in a virginal state.

If that was true, you can see why *The Sun*'s women felt duty-bound to help all those inexperienced lovers spice up their love-lives with lots of how-to-do-it sex. A series called 'The Sensuous Couple' featured a love charter which began with the advice: 'Always make love naked. Always make love with the light on.' And 'If a woman wants to be really active or to initiate lovemaking, then a man should let her.'

It was all pretty basic but it was still breaking new ground. The things your mother never told you had not previously been available for the price of your morning newspaper.

There was also sensational sex as in 'The Casanova Girls':

> Some break all the bedroom records with the number of lovers they have. Why do they do it? What motivates them? Do they ever think of the consequences? Will they ever find a man they can be happy with? And will he want them?

Then followed an interview with a twenty-one-year-old Swede headed: 'Man crazy? Not me, says the girl who's had 798 lovers.'

There was no outrage expressed at the fact she had started notching up her record score at the age of twelve. Sex in *The Sun* was always fun in those carefree days before AIDS. It was the era known as the 'permissive society' and *The Sun* made the most of it – there have even been suggestions that the paper *invented* it.

The Sun's first women's editor was Joyce Hopkirk, who left after twelve months to become the first British editor of *Cosmopolitan*, the magazine generally credited with being the first to acknowledge that women were as interested in sex as men. She was young, divorced and fancy-free and says: 'I was very interested in sex so the paper reflected that. But we were never squalid. It had to be saucy and fun.

'As for exploitation of women, there wasn't any. The atmosphere in the 'Pacesetters' department was that *we* ruled the world.'

There was not only sex on the women's pages, there was also shopping. Journalist Val Hudson, otherwise known to readers as Little Val the Housewives' Pal, used to expose fiddles and rip-offs in the weekly consumer column, 'Counterspy'.

That was how readers learned that stores' own-brands were produced in famous brand-name factories (a *Sun* exclusive at the time). They also learned about the 'Meat Cheats' when butcher-shop tricks were exposed. And they were made aware of how much of a frozen chicken was made up of just water. *Sun* exposure of stale foods for sale is credited with forcing shops to display a 'sell by' date on foodstuffs. A big feature on how the Common Market would affect the British shopper was quoted in the House of Commons by Shirley Williams, then Minister for Consumer Affairs.

But even consumer affairs were fun in *The Sun*. When mattresses were put to the test, a pair of newlyweds bounced their way round twenty different makes. When socks came under scrutiny, there was 'Everything you ever wanted to know about sox but were too darned tired to ask'.

There were serious issues for women as well. 'Women Who Die of Embarrassment' was an award-winning series on cervical cancer which was reproduced as a pamphlet in conjunction with the Women's National Cancer Control Campaign. There was also 'The Survivors', a follow-up series on women who had undergone treatment for breast cancer.

Right from the start, women readers loved *The Sun*. It introduced the principles of magazine journalism into newspapers and struck a chord immediately. It reflected a hitherto unrecognized fact that women could be as nudge-nudge and as outright bawdy about sex as men. It gave them a laugh.

'We created a climate for women to be brave and not conform to men's ideas of what they thought women wanted,' says Joyce Hopkirk.

'When we did funny, sexy things in the paper, women knew it was often tongue in cheek, they knew they weren't being patronized, that we were on their side.

'We were helped enormously by the fact that the men editing the paper loved women – in the nicest sense. It was an atmosphere where ideas could blossom because no one felt inhibited.

'Bernard and Larry were amazed how frank we all were about sex. I don't think they had heard women talk in such a frank way before and this definitely hit the spot with our readers.'

Larry Lamb says he is a feminist. When he was recruiting staff for the new *Sun* he hired as many women as he could. In fact, the Equal Opportunities Commission stepped in at one stage when *The Sun* advertised specifically for women journalists. There are still large numbers of women writers on the paper. Patsy Chapman, now editor of the *News of the World,* was deputy editor of *The Sun* for two years having been night editor before that. *The Sun* has had women writing on politics, economics, finance, racing.

Some of the best specialist reporting has been by women. There were memorable exposures of misery in an old people's home and life in a mental hospital, both by investigative reporter Jean Ritchie who had a chameleon-like talent for going undercover. Indeed, during the three weeks she spent as a cleaner at Friern Barnet Mental Hospital she was actually taken aside by the head cleaner and told she was 'supervisor material'.

It was probably because of the dust-up she had one morning over the way she cleaned a floor. Ritchie says, 'I was supposed to clean and polish half the floor of an enormous ward. But one day the woman who was supposed to do the other half didn't turn up, so I decided it was better for me to clean the whole area and leave out the polishing. I got ticked off for not just doing my share. I was told it was not my job to think.'

She had even more success when she posed as a member of the hippy convoy making its way to Stonehenge for the summer solstice. And it was not easy for this mother-of-three to turn herself into a dope-smoking drop-out.

'The first night when they were all sitting round the fire talking about 'the stones' I thought they meant the Rolling Stones,' she says. 'And I had real trouble being convincing when they passed the joints around because I've never smoked a cigarette.'

However, by the third day she had the hang of being a hippy so well she was giving interviews to Swedish TV, Dutch radio – and the *Daily Star*. Mischievously, she even begged money for phone calls from journalists: 'One television guy gave me a big lecture along the lines of "you people don't do yourselves any favours" etcetera. I said, "Oh go on, mate, you won't miss 10p out of your expenses."'

Ritchie did not fare so well when she joined the protesting women of Greenham Common. Her presence there was leaked to the *Guardian* and got a mention on Radio Four, so she had to pull out after one night. She wasn't sorry. She admits, 'I know they were peace campaigners but I don't feel they'd have been too peaceful towards me if they'd found out I was a *Sun* journalist.'

There are plenty of moments when it is risky to admit you're from *The Sun*, as writer Ruth Brotherhood discovered when she went to Majorca to report on troublesome young British holidaymakers.

'I bowled into a bar where there were a few lads larking around,' she says. 'And the moment I mentioned I was from *The Sun*, within seconds there were hundreds of guys leering and yelling, dropping their trousers and giving V-signs.

'In no time, the policed roared up – and grabbed me and the photographer. They bundled us into the back of their van and said they were going to charge us with inciting a riot. It took us about two hours to talk them out of it.'

Women were very often the writers of the highly stylized, pun-filled captions for Page Three pictures. When the pin-ups first went topless it was Larry Lamb's view that the choice of pictures should be such that 'the reasonable and tolerant majority' of women would not be offended. If his women journalists found a Page Three choice offensive in any way, he would not publish it.

No one can remember a difference of opinion over pin-ups between the editor and women writers. But *Sun* women writers did once make a highly effective protest against the more lurid pin-ups on some male office walls. On the side of a filing cabinet facing the door of the women feature writers' room they pinned up a collection of male nudes, mostly from German naturist magazines. This was known as 'the willie wall' and made male visitors noticeably blanch.

By far the biggest topic of women's interest in *The Sun* alongside sex has been slimming. For seventeen years the paper has been putting its readers and a whole range of showbiz, sporting, political and other personalities on diets. As Sally Ann Voak, the slimming editor for all those years, puts it, 'I've taken lorryloads of flab off the British public.'

Voak's enthusiasm knows no bounds. As she says, 'Slimming spans every emotion known to man or woman: greed, lust, the whole seven deadly sins.'

She once got the village of Broadbottom in Cheshire to take part in a slimming experiment by pinning notices on telegraph poles inviting the inhabitants to a meeting in the local pub that night. She reported:

> People in the beautiful Cheshire village of Broadbottom like a good laugh. Which is just as well – they are sitting targets for jibes about wobbly bits and fat bums.
>
> But now they have become so fed up with such deep-seated insults that ONE HUNDRED villagers out of a population of about 550 have decided to slim.

Six weeks later at a mass weigh-in, a loss of 1000 lbs was chalked up. Sally Ann jubilantly told readers:

> They've done it, folks! The beefy villagers of Broadbottom have triumphantly trimmed down and toned up. And today they could proudly rename their home SLIM-BOTTOM! In one of the greatest slimming experiments ever, the locals have taken the broad out of their own bottoms.

The Sun's slimming expert went on to do likewise with the inhabitants of the Wide Way, in Mitcham, Surrey: 'What do you do if you have a broad beam, a tubby tummy, and wobble when you walk? If you happen to live in a street called Wide Way, you blush every time someone asks your address!'

So she put twelve volunteers on the Cambridge Diet and monitored their efforts. The result: 'Does it work? You bet! The proof is in a dozen puddings – who are now a trifle slimmer than they were.'

Sun slimmers are game for anything. When Jim and Teresa Mombrun wrote to tell Sally it was their dream to be able to share a bath together, they probably did not have in mind a splash-in in the middle of a *Sun* photographic studio.

'RUB A DUB DUB, WE GET IN THE TUB' was the result of a ten-stone weight loss by Teresa, who had previously caused a flood if she bathed alone. Her carpenter husband had had to knock down a wall in the family bathroom so she could stand at the washbasin in comfort. After the Voak-supervised diet, Teresa and Jim were only too delighted to take the plunge in front of the cameras: 'The Sun made their dreams come true this week with a romantic tub-in – to celebrate Teresa's sud-sational weight loss'.

'THINDERELLA' was a spectacular Voak production in which she played Fairy Sunmother to a pair of plump sisters who she slimmed 'to fit their tight new pantos . . .'

> Once upon a time there were two fat, ugly sisters . . . And when they put on their 1987 Christmas gear ready to go to this year's ball, they looked just like a pair of plumpkins.
>
> The girls were just about to drown their sorrows with a food binge when up popped their Fairy Godmother – ME!'
>
> I decided to help the sisters to lose their lumps and bumps and get out of the dumps.
>
> And guess what? They are all living less-hippy ever after!

Edwina Currie has slimmed with Sally. So have Lord Prior and actor Paul Henry, otherwise known as Benny from 'Crossroads'. She even sent a diet to the Duke of York after *The Sun* published a particularly pudgy photograph of him, calling him The Duke of Pork.

Not the Duke of York's favourite picture of himself

The rather dated 'Pacesetters' title was dropped from *The Sun*'s women's features around the end of the Seventies. There was no special women's section for a number of years, in the belief that all features should be of interest to both sexes. You could tell a women-only piece from the fact that it usually started with the words 'Hey girls'.

But since the beginning of 1988 women readers have had their own weekly pull-out of features, 'Sun Woman', edited by Sue Carroll. It is full of 'emotional' features which concentrate on whole relationships and is worlds away from what's what under the duvet. There is an emphasis on health, slimming and fitness plus interviews with a mix of stars and *Sun* readers about how they deal with their emotional lives and crises.

'The days when everybody wondered what everyone else was doing between the sheets are over. We are more interested in how other women are motivated and why they react the way they do,' says Carroll, who reports a phenomenal response to the 'Emotions Doctor' who now gives advice in a weekly column. 'People are fascinated by why others feel the way they do.'

Former top model Jilly Johnson has talked about being fed up with being a mistress. Actor Colin Baker and his wife, Marion, gave a moving interview about how they eased the pain of a cot death. Readers have bared their souls to talk about being the victims of sexual abuse or losing loved ones.

Telephone counselling by trained experts has been offered to readers suffering specific troubles – for instance, battered wives. Sue Carroll feels strongly about helping as well as entertaining her readers. She was hugely gratified when a woman reader rang one morning, tearful with relief, to thank the paper for publishing a piece on what to do if someone in the family is choking.

'My daughter nearly choked to death and if I hadn't had that piece of paper I wouldn't have known what to do,' the woman said.

The woman's editor is also grateful to find her pages read by plenty of men. She gets at least twenty letters a week from hopeful hunks wanting to try their talents as Page Seven Fellas.

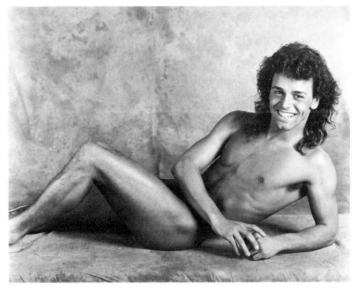

A hopeful hunk from the women's pages

It may seem strange that a newspaper which has prided itself on not having traditional women's pages should, for the first time, publish a whole section labelled 'Sun Woman'. The editor says that there are seven pages of 'Sunsport' in the paper every day, read by a minority of women, so why not give women their own pages once a week?

Sue Carroll thinks women are finally reaping the benefits of feminism. 'We've got a real role, jobs, our own money, the independence that goes with it. Women like to have their own voice and to know what other women are doing.

'You've only got to look at the vast expansion in the women's magazine market to know women have special interests which should be catered for.'

10. *No Stopping Wapping*

Sun journalists never dreamed that one day they would go to work behind barbed wire. But that happened on 25 January 1986, the day after *Sun* printers went on strike for the very last time.

On Friday 24 January everyone had turned up for work as usual in their grimy offices at 30 Bouverie Street, just off Fleet Street. But that evening they left that old familiar building with its giant, roman-numeralled clock hanging outside, carrying all their working possessions in black plastic binbags like a bunch of refugees. It was goodbye to The Street and hello Wapping.

A whole new world was about to be explored and not too many tears were shed into the champagne as writers, photographers, sub-editors and artists celebrated the end of an era before getting out their *London A-Z* guides and trying to discover exactly where Wapping was.

The move had been rumoured for a long time. After all, the plant had been waiting to be used out in the borough of Tower Hamlets for six years. Originally it had been planned as simply a press hall where the papers would be printed on modern machinery, a far cry from the antiquated machines and stifling subterranean print halls of Bouverie Street. The journalists, at least initially, were to be left where they were.

Rupert Murdoch had bowed to the unions from the very first

moments of *The Sun*. On the night of the launch, his wife Anna had to be made a temporary print union member before she could push the button for the presses to roll.

But it was seventeen years before he saw the chance of escaping the union shackles. A set of circumstances arose which gave him the break he needed. Eddie Shah was about to launch *Today*, the first national daily to be published without print union labour, in colour, on new-tech machines at a fraction of the cost of any of its rivals. And new legislation made it harder for workers to strike.

'I had the idea of making a dash for freedom with a non-Fleet Street work force eleven months before we moved,' Murdoch says. 'In the February we placed orders for computers and started organizing that dash.'

The idea was to use Wapping to publish a new paper, the *London Post*. But around Christmas 1985 there was mounting aggravation between *The Sun*'s printers and the management over the publication of the new title. No agreements could be reached with members of the two print unions (the National Graphical Association and the Society of Graphic and Allied Trades) over manning levels. If the unions would not come to terms, Murdoch knew there had to be a contingency plan.

'We realized that if we did the *Post* with non-NGA, non-NATSOPA labour, it would probably close down the other two places,' says Murdoch, referring to Bouverie Street and Grays Inn Road. That was why a 10 million dollar computer was assembled in secret in a South London warehouse by American and Australian technicians living in a 'safe house' in Belgravia. If plans for the *Post* broke down, he knew his only chance of enabling his other papers to survive was to print them in Wapping.

In many disputes over the years, the unions had wound up winners every time, simply by stopping the presses and walking out. As a result of these tactics, many *Sun* printers were paid double what most journalists took home and some had reduced their work load to the point where they were able successfully to do other jobs as well. Many were taxi drivers.

What were known as 'Spanish practices' – fiddles, to the rest of the world – were the name of the game as the print unions got away with murder. Overmanning reached crazy proportions as the unions insisted on seventeen men to each press, though they were efficiently manned by just four elsewhere. Truck drivers delivering *The Sun* insisted that two drivers and a loader were necessary to do the job over certain mileages. But only one driver went.

The print unions set the figure for *The Sun*'s print run and if the management wanted to print more copies, the men had to get more money. They also demanded 'special events' payments for big news stories like elections and royal weddings and 'compression' money for when a big news story broke late. There were cases where workers dodged tax by using false names like Mickey Mouse, Donald Duck and Roy Rogers to collect casual payments.

The fiddles were endless and any move to stop or curb them brought the threat of a strike. In every dispute, brute strength won out: the printers stopped the presses and, over the years, cost the company millions in lost papers. Until Wapping. The plant that had stood idle for years while unions wrangled over the severely reduced manpower needed for its high-tech machinery was now all geared up to go.

Despondent journalists knew, as soon as the printers downed tools on that wintry Friday in 1986, that their jobs were in jeopardy. They knew *something* was going on in Wapping but not whether it included them. But at 6.00pm that evening it was made clear by Kelvin MacKenzie. At a meeting in *The Sun* features room he made the following speech:

'Seven years ago, Rupert Murdoch decided to build a plant at Wapping, mainly because if the papers were going to be successful he felt *The Sun* and the *News of the World* wanted extra capacity. For six years he tried to persuade SOGAT and the NGA to join with him down at that plant. For six years they said no.

'Finally one of the branch secretaries at London Central, seeing the new plant, turned round and said, "The best thing you can do is blow this place up." At that point there seemed no further point in continuing to try to get the traditional unions to take part in what was obviously going to be the future. So off we went from there. And Mr Murdoch went on. And we completed it. And as you will see if you read the *Sunday Times* or watch "Panorama", various things had to be done in secret to get that plant into shape . . . because we had been at the end of blackmailing and bullying on every single pay round, every single piece of technology that we tried to introduce into this building. Every single time there was a threat that if we didn't turn it away they would shut us down.

'In a minute-to-minute industry, when they've got you by the balls, you've got to listen. Well, they haven't got us by the balls any more. The situation is simply this: the only people that matter any more are the journalists. There can't be papers without journalists and it is with this in mind that we are now going to make this momentous step from Bouverie Street down to Wapping . . . We need you. It is you that makes the paper. I personally want every single one of you, including those who are ideologically at the opposite end of the pole from me. I want every single one of you in Wapping.'

There was some discussion over what the journalists' position would be if they were thrown out of the National Union of Journalists, a situation which seemed likely if they disobeyed their union's instructions to support the printworkers and go on strike.

MacKenzie told them: 'What the NUJ has done for you could safely fit up a gnat's arse. What you have done for yourselves has been incredible . . . I must think of becoming a member . . .'

With very few exceptions, the 200 journalists voted to go. *Sun* journalists were still bitter over the lack of support from NGA and SOGAT members about eighteen months earlier when printworkers stomped cheerfully through their picket lines during a journalists' strike. It made it much easier to bear the shouts of 'Scab!' as they walked, bussed and drove their way into Wapping.

After the grot, squalour and noise of Bouverie Street, the vast open-plan editorial floor at Wapping was calm, clean and very high-tech: more like a movie set than a reporters' room. As royal writer Judy Wade said, 'I feel as if I'm starring in "Lou Grant".'

There were reunions all over the place. A small number of sub-editors who had mysteriously 'disappeared' in the past few months suddenly reappeared among the computers and potted palms at Wapping. It was not a total surprise. Rumours of their whereabouts had led to the explanation that they had gone off with 'the Wapping cough'.

David Banks, *The Sun's* executive editor in charge of the new technology equipment and training at Wapping, was one who had been out of sight for a long time. He had been in America studying computer systems and then at Wapping practising dummy runs with *Sun* copy which was secretly faxed from Bouverie Street before being sent down to the old composing room for traditional setting.

'Everything was being fed to us at Wapping and we were right up with it. When the printers pulled the plug, we were ready,' he said later. He was also on the receiving end of calls from Kelvin MacKenzie while the journalists decided whether or not Wapping was for them.

'Every time he walked out of their meeting he'd phone me,' said Banks. 'He'd say, "I fucked it. I lost my temper." Then he would be very down and saying, "I think it's me, there's too much animosity."

'I had no compunction about what we did at Wapping – and I am a strong believer in unions. But I knew the journalists would come. I was reassuring Kelvin, "Our guys know all about the Mickey Mice and the Donald Ducks."

'Suddenly he called and shouted, "We're coming down. The journalists are on their way!"'

One of the first people he greeted was executive features editor Wendy Henry, who entered the newsroom followed by messenger boys carrying about half a dozen typewriters.

'You won't need those here,' Banks told her. She replied, 'Journalists will always need typewriters, babes.'

What they have occasionally used them for in Wapping is doorstops.

But as journalists struggled to grasp new computer skills and all was fairly calm inside the six-storey building only a few hundred yards from the Tower of London, there was often pandemonium in the street outside. On The Highway, despite assurances of peaceful picketing from national leaders of the printers' unions, ugly scenes often erupted as pickets hurled abuse and missiles.

It was not unusual to look out from the plant in the middle of the afternoon and see, hidden in a side street, a phalanx of mounted police in full riot gear, ready to move against the shouting hordes in the street. Mostly they just yelled, 'Scab! Scab!' from behind their steel barricades every time a person or vehicle entered the plant. But sometimes there was mob violence, often engineered by outsiders who came in as secondary pickets and were spoiling for a fight.

What whipped them to fever pitch was the sight of the giant TNT lorries rolling out through the security gates of 'Fortress Wapping' carrying their loads of newspapers. On Saturday nights, the trucks carrying the *News of the World* and *The Sunday Times* were targets for some of the worst violence, with crowds of 5000 and more clashing with police. On one occasion there was a crowd of 13,000 which police said they could not have stopped should the mob have blockaded the plant. On that night, 168 of the 1000 police on duty were injured.

Editor Kelvin MacKenzie and his deputy, David Shapland, each had a strapping 'minder' to accompany them in and out of work. People with cars just wound up their windows, turned up their radios and sailed through the picket lines as if they were not there. Some chose to brave it on foot because it made them feel less intimidated. But large numbers of the work force found it easiest to arrive at Wapping via what were known as the 'scab-wagons' – coaches with wire guards over the windows and drawn curtains.

These coaches picked up workers at different destinations each day, to avoid being ambushed or sabotaged by pickets. It was all very cloak-and-dagger.

The bus would pull up and people would suddenly swarm out of doorways, cafés, shops and subways to leap aboard. Then, at the gates of Wapping, a security guard would step inside and check everyone's security pass before waving the bus on.

It was not an enjoyable experience, somewhere between being checked into prison and a run in a gerbil's cage. But it was practical at the time.

And there were some laughs. The printers, who used to be known as 'inkies' in Fleet Street jargon, became known as the Incas – as opposed to the Aztecs, the journalists' name for the Americans from Atex, the computer experts there to make sure the system worked. 'We used to be run by the Incas, now it's the Aztecs,' was the line.

One of the 'Aztecs', a jolly lady from Chicago, came in very puzzled one morning and asked a sub-editor, 'What's this "scab" they're all yelling outside?'

'It's what you guys call a black-leg,' he told her. But she was still mystified. So he put it more plainly: 'It's someone who keeps working when everyone else is on strike.'

'Oh yeah?' she said. 'We just call 'em assholes.'

The picketing lasted just over a year before the barbed wire and the barricades came down. There were some regrettable incidents, including death threats. But by and large it was a bloodless revolution.

The unions had never lost a single fight in *The Sun*'s history, so when they walked out of Bouverie Street on their final Friday they thought they could not lose. What they were being asked was to agree to a no-strikes deal to work at Wapping.

'They couldn't concede they'd lost the fight. Brenda Dean (SOGAT leader) couldn't get it through to them. Instead of spending their time at the gates at Wapping, they should have been locking up lifetime jobs with other newspapers,' Murdoch says now.

'Right up till the end, we thought we'd start another paper very like *Today* OR bring the other titles down. If the unions had agreed to our request that time, we would have stayed where we were.'

The unions simply could not face the facts of late twentieth century publishing and the technological revolution.

'We tried to persuade them to come to terms with the whole thing,' Murdoch says. 'But we knew once we had one truck of papers out the gate at Wapping, we'd have won.'

11. *Nobody's Perfect*

All newspapers make mistakes. Unfortunately *The Sun* has gained a reputation for making more than any other. The truth, of course, is different: in its twenty years of existence, *The Sun* has made no more and no less mistakes than most of its rivals. It's just that *The Sun*'s have been more newsworthy.

Other papers get things wrong and the public hardly notices. But *The Sun* has dropped clangers which were so monumental that they made headlines themselves.

Who but *The Sun* could have landed itself with a record one million pound damages bill over untrue stories about Elton John? Who but *The Sun* could have been sued by the Queen? And then paid Her Majesty £100,000 in damages.

One popular myth is that *The Sun* gets some kind of perverse satisfaction out of being the black sheep of journalism. In fact, nothing could be further from the truth.

Editor Kelvin MacKenzie says, 'I hate it when we get something wrong. It spoils my whole day. And whoever is responsible for a mistake in the paper knows he or she is in for a roasting from me.'

Even a one-paragraph correction tucked away at the foot of a column will have caused a lot of aggravation in the office. Imagine the shouting that will have gone on over the Elton John affair.

It was the biggest SORRY that *The Sun* has ever had to say: in 2¼ inch high letters on the front page, alongside a smiling photo of Elton and a story revealing the incredible amount of damages to be paid.

But while it will go down as the most expensive libel blunder in British newspaper history, *The Sun* is determined that it must be the last mega-mistake in its own short history.

MacKenzie says if he had his life over again, the Elton John saga would never happen. He admits it was his biggest mistake. He says, 'I felt a great sense of shame that Elton John had to suffer in that way, and I felt a great sense of shame that readers would think a lot less of *The Sun* because of it.

'The truth about the whole sorry business is that *The Sun* was taken in, hook, line and sinker by a very plausible young man who turned out to be an expert liar.

'In a way we deserved to suffer. If you pay people like rent boys or prostitutes, who live by deceit and criminality, you should be wary about believing them.

'One of the most hurtful things people say about *The Sun* is that you can't believe a word we publish because we make it all up. Nothing could be further from the truth. We get enough bizarre, wacky, weird, oddball and almost unbelievable stories that are 100 per cent genuine without having to stoop so low as to invent them. Our news desk gets dozens of calls every day from people tipping us off about stories. Money is not the motive in many cases – some of the best stories have come anonymously from callers who hang up without giving their name and address.

'Every tip we get is checked out thoroughly by a reporter. Nothing is put in the paper before vigorous checks have been made. But one of the dangers of being in the newspaper business is that occasionally you get set up by someone who pulls off a very clever hoax.

'That doesn't just happen to *The Sun*, of course. Remember when the *Daily Express* "found" the Nazi war criminal Martin Bormann in South America? That was a clever hoax.

'Remember when the *Daily Mail* had to publish a most grovelling apology after being fooled into printing untrue allegations that British

The Sun *drops a clanger*

Leyland had an improper slush fund? Remember the highly reputable German magazine which was tricked into publishing Hitler's secret diaries, which later turned out to be one of the most brilliant hoaxes ever? The list is endless of newspapers which have printed in good faith what later turned out to be a lie.

'The Sun is no different from any other paper. When we publish something that later turns out to be wrong, we feel foolish. We feel angry. We feel ashamed that we have allowed ourselves to be taken in.

'Interestingly, our readers did not give us any flak at all over Elton John. Their only reaction was shock at the size of the settlement. Many felt it was odd that a man's reputation appeared to be worth more than his life, if damages awarded to accident victims were anything to go by.'

For MacKenzie it has been a time to count not just the cost but the morality of it all. 'We make mistakes,' he admits, 'but it would be surprising if we didn't, publishing as we do some 20,000 items of news each year. And by God, we pay for those mistakes.

'If you are involved in a car crash and can never work again, you may get £500,000 in damages. If you're an actress and aspersions are made against you in a newspaper, you walk away in good health with a bloody fortune. It's wrong, wrong, wrong.

'We wish we didn't make mistakes and our readers wish we didn't. But the idea that The Sun is like some rampaging army searching the sewers of life for front page stories is ridiculous.'

Not everybody sues, of course. Many write to the newspaper industry's independent watchdog, the Press Council. The Sun had the dubious honour of topping the Press Council's complaints league in 1987, when twenty-two complaints were considered by the Council. In fifteen of them, The Sun was judged to have been in the wrong.

In 1988, only six complaints against The Sun were upheld and one was deemed to be only partially proven. That is still seven complaints too many for the editor's liking, but in the context of the 20,000 news items published that year the number is very small.

The Sun has made a lot of enemies because of its forthright opinions and brash presentation. They relish every opportunity to make capital out of the best-selling *Sun*'s misdoings. The *Daily Mirror,* in particular, envies *The Sun*'s success and frequently baffles most of its readers by devoting huge leader columns to *The Sun*'s activities.

Getting stories wrong has not been the only source of complaints against *The Sun.* Bad taste has given cause for protest, though usually not from readers but from people who may have seen a headline on a poster or in a newsagent's shop.

One loud chorus of complaint came in 1987 when *The Sun*'s front page carried a picture of Katherine Bowes-Lyon with an exclusive story headlined 'QUEEN'S COUSIN LOCKED IN MADHOUSE, 46-year nightmare of abandoned Kate'.

The story said that Miss Bowes-Lyon had been shunned and shut away in a mental hospital and that her mentally handicapped sister Nerissa had been buried in a pauper's grave the year before. The use of the word 'madhouse' offended many people – but then *The Sun* has always believed in calling a spade a spade.

Her Majesty the Queen's wrath has been visited on *The Sun* on several occasions, including an historic first in 1983 when she took legal action to stop publication of an exclusive behind-the-scenes peek at Buckingham Palace.

The proposed report was totally accurate – it was just that the Queen was not amused. The High Court granted her request and the article was duly censored.

Prince Philip was not amused, either, when *The Sun* published the contents of a private letter he had written to the Royal Marines on the subject of Prince Edward's resignation. The personal letter to Sir Michael Wilkins, Commandant-General of the Marines, was obtained without authority, causing the Queen to threaten to go to court against *The Sun* yet again. This time Prince Philip won an estimated £25,000 damages to be paid to a charity of his choice.

The royals' next wrangle with *The Sun* came in October 1988 over the famous family photo headlined 'THE QUEEN BEA', of the Duchess of York with her baby daughter on her knee, flanked by the Queen and the Queen Mother. A young girl at the laboratory where the photo was being processed owned up to selling the snap which was published in *The Sun*. The Queen managed to extract £100,000 from *The Sun* in damages for this invasion of her private life.

There was also royal rage in December 1987 when *The Sun* broke an embargo on the Queen's New Year's Honours List by twenty-four hours. In a front-page story it revealed that two hereos of the Zeebrugge disaster were being awarded George Medals.

The list, issued annually by the prime minister's office, is given to all newspapers, radio and television stations in advance so they are able to prepare background stories. *The Sun*'s punishment for this 'crime' was a heavy wigging from the prime minister's press secretary, Bernard Ingham, who called the paper's action 'disgraceful'.

But *The Sun* is unrepentant. Kelvin MacKenzie says, '*The Sun* is not clubbable. You wouldn't want *The Sun* to belong to your club and we certainly don't want to belong to the Establishment club. Therefore every so often the paper for the working men and women of this country is going to do something a bit off the wall.'

Most complaints against *The Sun* are not dealt with in the courts or by the Press Council. They land fair and square on the desk of managing editor Kenneth Donlan, newly named as the British press's first ombudsman.

A large number of the complaints he receives are because people disagree with a point of view published in the paper. 'It happens a great deal with stories about race and ethnic origin,' he says. 'Many are dealt with readily and easily by a letter or exchange of views. Some are settled by our agreeing on a correction or apology in the paper. A comparatively small number are adjudicated by the Press Council.'

He finds it more than mildly annoying that a lot of the flak sent in *The Sun*'s direction comes from people who don't even read the paper. 'Snobs who never read the paper but have an anti-*Sun* bias write and complain about our front page after seeing it on TV. They don't read *The Sun* and don't want to let our readers reason for themselves.'

12. *Nothing Exceeds Like Success*

The Sun's soaraway success is a puzzle to a lot of people, including its own journalists. Even the editor says that intellectualizing *The Sun*'s phenomenal appeal is not an easy trick. There is no magic formula. The paper just sells, sell, sells.

Critics say the reason is simple: it appeals to the lowest common denominator. If they mean that *The Sun* has an appeal that reaches most of the people most of the time, they are probably right. It is still hard to pin down what that appeal is.

If it was obvious, others would copy it immediately and, presumably, score the same success rate as *The Sun*. But others, most notably the *Daily Star*, have tried to copy and have failed dismally. There is clearly more to the top-selling tabloid than just boobs and bingo.

The present editor, Kelvin MacKenzie says frankly, 'I don't know why it's so successful. I'm never quite sure what the formula is. The only thing that makes me smile is when our competitors copy what they *think* is the formula. When other guys try to come up with the ingredients our readers like and are loyal to, it is hopeless.'

He puts lack of pomposity high among the reasons people like *The Sun*. 'Our natural reactions to life appear to be the readers' natural reactions. There is a partnership there. We are not talking down to them and they seem to like us.

'A lot of great newspapers, the *Daily Express*, the *Daily Mirror*, who used to sell in huge quantities, sell much less today because they became self-satisfied. We like to think we don't take our readers for granted and we are very grateful they go out and buy us every day.'

MacKenzie thinks it is easier for journalists to put across the Conservative way of life than to sell socialism: 'It is very tough to readers of a socialist tabloid to have journalists who earn £30,000 to £40,000 a year and live in £200,000 houses writing about how disgraceful it is that council houses are being sold off. We don't have that problem.

A lot of *Sun* journalists are a bit of a surprise to people expecting a sub-human species like the pigs representing *Sun* people on 'Spitting Image'. About half are graduates, many from Oxford or Cambridge. Some went to public school – including Eton. But there are also school drop-outs, ex-nurses, ex-dancers, all ranging in age from twenty-two to the late fifties. They also have exotic outside interests, for instance letters editor Sue Cook sings opera, assistant editor Chris Davies is a professional magician. In fact, a fairly wide slice of life turns up daily on the *Sun* editorial floor.

The main area in which they differ from other journalists on other papers is in having to justify their jobs to critics and non-*Sun* readers. Everyone likes to take a dig: '*Sun* journalist? But they don't have words in the *Sun*, do they?' Or: 'Wouldn't you rather work on the *Telegraph/Guardian/Times?*' ('They couldn't afford me,' is the answer to that one.)

Kelvin MacKenzie says: 'We are in favour of readers being as successful as we are, to do the best they can. If they can't be successful, let's hope their children can work towards independence.'

He also thinks *The Sun*'s good fortune was in being the right paper at the right time: 'We caught a rip-tide, I think we are part of a popular movement,'

In 1978, the year *The Sun* overtook the *Mirror* to become Britain's biggest-selling daily paper, Larry Lamb gave his recipe for success to the *UK Press Gazette*. He said, 'Never be boring, never be ashamed to entertain, never assume that what is dull must be important, never confuse big black type and bold pictures with irresponsibility and never assume that the product must be tailored to pander to the prejudices, real or imagined, of readers.'

Nine years later, on *The Sun*'s eighteenth birthday, Larry Lamb, now Sir Larry, wrote in the paper:

> WHY does The Sun remain such a soaraway success 18 years on?
>
> The Sun was – and is – as unpredictable as it is irrepressible. It refuses to be pigeon-holed.
>
> We acknowledged what many journalists were at that time anxious to forget – that the basic interests of the human race are not in politics, philosophy or economics but in things like food and money, sex and crime, football and television.
>
> But we did not deal with these things to the exclusion of all others . . .
>
> We tried ceaselessly to make The Sun a newspaper which CARED, and a newspaper which MATTERED. A newspaper which got it FIRST, and got it RIGHT. A newspaper for PEOPLE, not for Fleet Steet.

Rupert Murdoch, who says that Larry Lamb and his staff 'gave it sizzle' and who admired Kelvin MacKenzie for 'his honesty and his drive for better stories' has this to say about the success of his most notorious newspaper: 'It understands its readers, their interests and their hopes and values. It is wonderfully edited and sub-edited, the language in it is straightforward. We have very strong trends of subbing, of boldness.

'I do think we speak for middle-England commonsense and we understand working-class values. It's a mixture of morality and hedonism: it sounds contradictory but we want them to have a good time yet have very strong values.'

Sun editors Lamb, Shrimsley and MacKenzie are strongly in agreement over the key to *The Sun*'s success being in the personality and extraordinary ability of its proprietor.

MacKenzie says, 'Rupert's the genius. It's his business and he knows it backwards. I don't know anybody who can sum up a paper as quickly and professionally as he can. I could name you proprietors who wouldn't know a great paper if it jumped up and bit their arse.'

Shrimsley says Murdoch is the first British newspaper owner since Lord Northcliffe to be a total newspaper man. 'He knows what every bit is for and how much it costs. He once said to me, "If you sent me a Xerox – do you know it costs 26p."

'He'll ask, "What do you need all these people for?" To which the answer is, "They don't work here. They just came in out of the rain."

'But there isn't anyone else like him. He doesn't need approval, he doesn't need cocktails with royalty, cosy lunches with peers. He is a relentless worker and he has no vanity – if he walks into a room and no one recognizes him it doesn't worry him.

'He was once having lunch with me and Larry Lamb and Rupert and I arrived first. The wine waiter asked if we would like a drink and Rupert said, "Yes thanks, we'll have a bottle of the house white."

'The waiter, who clearly didn't know him, looked down his nose and said, "I don't think Mr Lamb would like that, sir."'

News editor Tom Petrie says opportunism is the secret of why *The Sun* shines. 'We know what to go for and we know what our readers like when a situation presents itself. We have an extraordinary sense of when to go for the bizarre or the oddball.'

He also thinks *Sun* executives work harder than those elsewhere. Petrie says that because his editor works extremely hard it sets the tone for the rest. They don't dissolve into the pub at one o'clock 'like people on some other papers'.

Indeed, when Kelvin MacKenzie first took over at *The Sun*, he sent a memo to editorial staff which read:

> I am disgusted at the length of your lunch hours. Two hour breaks do not do this newspaper, your country or yourselves a favour. It is no wonder that Britain is rapidly turning into a Third World nation, if, when we do arrive at work we do

anything but work. I will take severe disciplinary action if I have to raise this subject of long lunch hours again.

A former *Sun* executive says, '*The Sun* is not an easy place to work. You are building your own pressure, piling pressure on yourself like you do in a top soccer team. At *The Sun* there is this feeling, "We won yesterday and we are going to win again today". There's a terrifying momentum built up. And Kelvin never rests. He is never away from the job and expects the same of his executives.

'We all at times loathed the pressure and the acrimony. Loads of hateful things were being said, there were bitter disputes, hasty decisions and HUGE BOLLOCKINGS. It's like the *Bounty* without the mutiny: there were always rumours from the fo'c'sle but no mutiny.'

It's hard to say who had the hardest job of the only three editors *The Sun* has had in the past twenty years: Larry Lamb, Bernard Shrimsley (Larry's deputy from day one, who edited the paper from 1972 to 1975) or Kelvin MacKenzie. Lamb and Shrimsley had the mammoth job of turning a failed, lack-lustre product into a slick bestseller. MacKenzie has the equally daunting job of keeping *The Sun* it its number one spot. When he became editor it was just before the launch of bingo and he said then, 'If sales shoot up I'll never know if it was me or bingo.'

The other two at least knew it was something they were doing right that sent sales soaring from a depressing 800,000 when they took it on, to 1.5 million after 100 issues, 2,810,000 at the end of three years, 3 million after four years and 4 million-plus when it took the top-of-the-tabloids title from the *Daily Mirror* after nine years. Larry Lamb always reckoned they would have done it much sooner if it had not been for print union restrictions. He once said he 'could not remember a time, not for years and years, when I have been able to produce precisely the newspaper I want to produce, on time, and had the print order filled, for ten consecutive days'.

Since the paper's move to Wapping, all that has changed. Kelvin MacKenzie certainly gets the newspaper he wants to produce.

In the beginning, *The Sun*'s climb to the top was very much designed in terms of what the *Daily Mirror* was doing wrong. It did not take expensive market research to work out that the *Mirror* had lost its sense of fun and was going for grey respectability. They wanted to appeal to the left-wing intellectuals as well as the masses. This explained why, at the time the fun-filled *Sun* hit the streets, the *Mirror* was boring its old readers with a heavy news pull-out known as 'Mirrorscope.'

The Sun promoted itself silly on television while the *Daily Mirror* insisted on believing that TV commercials did not sell newspapers. It also aimed for women readers by giving them the first raunchy women's pages in Fleet Street and acknowledging the new permissive Britain.

Rupert Murdoch still measures *The Sun* against the *Daily Mirror*. Every day, wherever he is in the world, he reads both papers. And sometimes he thinks the *Mirror* is the better one.

'They have good days and we have good days. Sometimes we have really good runs and outshine them for a month on end. But they've got a problem, they are very narrowed by their traditional political stance which is dated now. When they fall into a hole, we are able to outshine them for weeks. When they outshine us, it's only for a day or two,' he reckons.

Ex-*Sun* man David Banks thinks explaining the *Sun*'s success is a bit like trying to put into words the extraordinary success of The Beatles. 'A sociologist once said their rhythm was that of the heart-beat. The *Sun*'s rhythm is jungle drums – it's provocative, cheeky, exciting. You've got to mix it with *The Sun*. Love it or loathe it, everyone has an opinion about it.

'I see it as a branch of showbiz. It recognized for the first time the need for entertaining the reading public. The pages even *look* entertaining, rather like the front of a theatre, all stars and bright lights beckoning you inside. There's so much glitz and razzamatazz about *The Sun*.'

For Kelvin MacKenzie, one gauge of success is being slammed by both right- and left-wing critics. 'When we get attacked in the House of Commons by both the Tories and Labour I know we must be doing something right.'

The Sun's attackers certainly do cover the political spectrum. From Edward Heath to Tony Benn, from the *Sunday Express* to the *Guardian*, they have all taken a turn at *Sun*-bashing.

Take Labour's deputy leader Roy Hattersley, who has vowed to try to bring in laws to break up News International, the company which publishes *The Sun* among other titles. 'It is Rupert Murdoch who has dragged the other tabloids downmarket, who has blurred the line between news and comment. It is Rupert Murdoch who requires his employees to toe the Tory line . . . who broke the print unions. The Murdoch newspaper empire has to be broken up.'

The *Sunday Express*, in a column item about Myra Hindley and *The Sun*, spat, 'That tawdry little journal, *The Sun*, written for morons by morons, seldom adds anything to the nation's knowledge.'

Michael Foot, when he was leader of the House of Commons, told the House, 'The *Express*, *The Sun*, and most of the others are an absolute disgrace to journalism in this country.'

An *Observer* columnist moaned, 'Where would I be without *The Sun*? The nation as a whole would be better off, but I'd be lost as I'd have to find something else to hate.'

Womens's Lib champion Germaine Greer was an early attacker of *The Sun* and other Rupert Murdoch titles for their use of female pin-ups. 'He has subverted the morals and the quality of the working class in the most cynical fashion,' she said.

Moors murderer Ian Brady complained to the BBC about his picture being taken. 'The press succeeded in getting some new ones, including a full-length one, in of all hated papers, *The Sun*.'

The *Sunday Mirror* suggested this definition of the paper: 'The Sun – a newspaper worthy only for cutting into little squares and hanging in the outside privy'.

Lord Longford said, 'I have a very low opinion of *The Sun*. Their persecution of Myra Hindley is just about the most vindictive thing in the history of journalism.'

(The good Lord once rang editor Kelvin MacKenzie when he felt the paper had been particularly mean to Myra. His opening words were: 'I wonder how you can sleep at nights?' Said the editor: 'I sleep a lot better for knowing that Myra Hindley is safely locked up.')

Edward Heath, responding to a *Sun* leader which accused him of bitterness and of sniping at Mrs Thatcher, wrote a long letter published in *The Sun* which ended: '*The Sun* is the lackey of its financial bosses. Poor *Sun*.'

Tony Benn, referring to *The Sun*'s coverage of the Falklands War, said, 'These ideas which were associated with the Fascism of the 1920s and 30s are now appearing day after day in *The Sun*.'

A Norfolk vicar, writing in his parish magazine, said, 'I cannot comprehend a Christian taking home *The Sun*.'

A feature article in the *Independent* claimed: '. . . it is nonsense for *The Sun* to argue that its resilient sales prove that it is a good newspaper.'

But the *Daily Mirror* is the biggest *Sun*-basher of all. Under the headline 'THE HARLOT OF FLEET STREET', it devoted a full page to one attack. '*The Sun*, a coarse and demented newspaper,' is how it began. It went on to say: 'It has long been a tawdry newspaper. But since the Falklands crisis began it has fallen from the gutter to the sewer.'

Again, the *Mirror*: '*The Sun* is a boastful newspaper. But when it boasts it is the cheapest national newspaper then for once it tells the truth.'

Editor MacKenzie is not too bothered by the bashers. He says, 'In essence, we don't take any notice of our critics. If we changed our newspaper into the sort of paper they would like, we'd have the sort of circulation they have.

'We get attacked for being successful. If Sainsbury's were selling a kind of sausage which had people queuing at the door, people would say, "These guys are geniuses."

'Well, *we* make a great sausage and everyone says, what a disgusting sausage, who's the swine who produced this sausage?

'People who don't buy *The Sun* just don't understand it.'

13. *Twenty Things*

AND HERE ARE TWENTY THINGS YOU MAY STILL BE FASCINATED TO KNOW ABOUT *THE SUN*

1. The editor, Kelvin MacKenzie, is famous for having only one O-level, variously reported as being for art, technical drawing and woodwork. In fact, it was for English literature, the only subject he passed of the seven he attempted as a student of Alleyns School, Dulwich. 'I don't know how I got that – I only read the crammer, I never read the books,' he says. A year later he sat the same seven subjects at Brixton College and failed the lot. Technically, he has no O-levels.

2. As you step into the *Sun* newsroom, a sign over the door tells you: 'You Are Now Entering Sun Country'. Inside, another sign reminds reporters: 'News is anything that makes the reader say, "Gee whizz!"'

3. When legendary boozer Oliver Reed rang to complain about a story in *The Sun*, editor Kelvin MacKenzie enraged him further by picking up the phone and saying, 'Alcoholics Anonymous.'

4. Pint-sized Page Three girl, Samantha Fox, now a singing superstar, once said she would only cross picket lines at Wapping in a tank. It was arranged. As she rolled through the security gates, the news and picture editors turned out in combat gear to salute her.

5. When the paper launched a 'Hop Off You Frogs' campaign against the French, two photographers from *Paris Match* chased *Sun* editor MacKenzie round his office – but never got his picture.

6. Sir Larry Lamb's real first name is Albert but he was nick-named Larry after a small woolly inhabitant of 'Toytown'.

7. Australian Evonne Goolagong, the former Wimbledon champion, was once shown naked in a *Sun* cartoon, for which the paper was censured by the Press Council.

8. There is a theory that all chauffeurs read *The Sun*. Larry Lamb once said, 'Just about everyone of influence, asked if he reads *The Sun*, seems to claim that he sees it from time to time because his chauffeur buys it.'

9. *The Sun* was the first newspaper to give away a one-million-pound bingo prize. However, its second million-pound winner collected the prize as a result of a fraud and ended up being dealt with by the law.

10. A lot of readers were upset over a *Sun* photograph accompanying a story about the Sicilian mafia, which showed a man's head on the seat of a car. They would have been more upset if they had heard a picture desk man say, 'It's a long way to go just for a head shot.'

11. The man who built Wapping was known as Bert the Butcher – Bert Hardy, News Group Newspapers' chief executive till his departure in 1978. It was his idea to find new premises where *The Sun* could be printed because the Bouverie Street plant was too small and becoming rundown. He says now, 'If Rupert hadn't sacked me, I think I would have persuaded the unions to keep their jobs and move to Wapping – and the history of Fleet Street would have been different. Rupert was quite right to fire me.'

12. A *Sun* reporter once got sent to an auction of showbiz memorabilia to buy 'Kenny Everett's tits' – the false front worn by Kenny in his TV show. He got them by arranging an anonymous bid so other reporters would not know what *The Sun* was up to.

13. When a *Sun* editorial advocated sending in the RAF against Iran, should the 'mad mullahs' harm British author Salman Rushdie, one *Sun* journalist thought it a bit over the top. 'It'd be different if it was Leslie Thomas,' he explained.

14. When Princess Michael's cat went missing, a *Sun* reporter was sent after it in a pith helmet and carrying a net. '*The Sun* is best for mews and pictures,' read the caption above his story.

15. When the halfpenny coin was phased out, *Sun* readers were asked to save their coppers in a 'Tiddlers for Toddlers' campaign. The overwhelming response resulted in a collection of £1.5 million pounds which *The Sun* distributed among twenty children's charities.

16. The five finalists in *The Sun*'s 'British Beer Belly' competition were a thirsty lot who could all down a pint in one gulp. When they were taken to the pub to quench their thirst after a photo session the photographer had to send an SOS to the office for more money. They drank sixty pints – and that was just a warm-up.

17. The paper's 'Zeebrugge Disaster Fund' raised about £1.3 million pounds, of which £700,000 came from sales of a recording of 'Let It Be' by a chorus of stars who all did it for nothing.

18. When *The Sun* was snapping a group of royal lookalikes outside Buckingham Palace, the heavily pregnant model impersonating the then-pregnant Princess of Wales went into labour.

19. One Page Three girl called Tula was a stunning beauty who turned out to be an ex-seaman called Terry who had changed his sex.

20. In the early days of *The Sun*, artists had to paint bikini tops on the Page Three girls for the Spanish edition of the paper. Ironically, quite a few of those topless pictures had been taken in Spain where photographers went on location.